Ronald Sutherland Gower

The Figure Painters of Holland (1880)

Ronald Sutherland Gower

The Figure Painters of Holland (1880)

ISBN/EAN: 9783743321670

Manufactured in Europe, USA, Canada, Australia, Japa

Cover: Foto ©Thomas Meinert / pixelio.de

Manufactured and distributed by brebook publishing software
(www.brebook.com)

Ronald Sutherland Gower

The Figure Painters of Holland (1880)

" The whole world without Art would be one great wilderness."

THE FIGURE PAINTERS
OF HOLLAND

BY LORD RONALD GOWER

Trustee of the National Portrait Gallery

LONDON

SAMPSON LOW, MARSTON, SEARLE, & RIVINGTON

CROWN BUILDINGS, FLEET STREET

1880

LONDON: R. CLAY, SONS, AND TAYLOR,
BREAD STREET HILL, E.C.

CONTENTS.

LIST OF ILLUSTRATIONS.

FIGURE PAINTERS OF HOLLAND.

INTRODUCTION.

LORD BACON'S definition, "*Ars est homo additus naturæ*," applies, we think, more to the painters of Holland than to the artists of any other school. Out of the sixteen chosen for this volume as representative men, two only, Honthorst and Van der Helst, are figure or portrait painters only. The fourteen others—although we think only of Terborch's and Mieris's courtiers and ladies, of Steen's and Brouwer's peasants and yokels, of Maes's and Dou's kitchen-maids and children—were, one and all, artists not only proficient in the delineation of faces and figures, but also excellent in the more difficult qualities of the painter's art : their talent in the representation of lights and shades has rarely been equalled, and never been surpassed

At first sight it may appear that any account, however slight, of the Dutch figure painters without including the names of Rembrandt,* the most celebrated of them all,

---

* Biographies of Rembrandt and Frans Hals have already appeared in this series.

and Frans Hals, perhaps the most original of the Dutch
Masters of portrait painting, would have but little interest;
and when the writer first took the task in hand, he felt as
if he had been asked to speak of our English portrait
painters without mentioning Reynolds and Gainsborough,
or of the English landscape painters without including
Turner and Constable. But the Dutch School of painting is
quite an exceptional one, and the great interest attaching to
these artists of Holland is that they were something much
more remarkable than merely painters of figures. Isack
van Ostade's out-of-door scenes would be delightful landscapes, even if the peasants that enliven them were
omitted, and Wouwerman's breezy skies and soft distances,
even if the huntsmen and hounds could gallop out of his
pictures, would remain among the best landscapes that
have ever been painted.

It is this almost universal power of painting nature, a
nature animated by human actors, that makes the works
of these old Dutch artists so precious to the collector and
amateur, and so valuable to the student and artist, and
it is that which elicited from our greatest artist, Joshua
Reynolds, the opinion that "painters should go to the
Dutch School to learn the art of painting, as they would
go to a Grammar School to learn languages."

There is nothing more instructive or curious in the
history of art than to trace the rapid rise of the Dutch
School, its wonderful reign, and its rapid decline. The
Dutch figure painters did not appear till after the War of
Independence, when the portion of the Netherlands, now
Belgium, became the Spanish Netherlands, as distinct
from the Northern Netherlands, which then proudly took
the name of the United Provinces. Freed from the
tyranny of the Romish Church, this newly enfranchised

country produced, as it were by magic, a fresh and a national art, one that was essentially domestic.

We can trace even in the works of the early Flemish painters, such as Massys of Antwerp, and Lucas van Leyden, a tendency to paint domestic subjects ; and when once freed from the obligations of painting for the clergy and the church, the true bent of the national art among the Dutch at once declared itself.

While Rubens was buying indulgences from the priests by painting pictures for churches, Rembrandt would take some old Jew from out the slums of Amsterdam, and paint a portrait of the old Shylock with as much care as Rubens would have bestowed on St. Peter or St. Paul.

No more priests, no more church pictures for the painters of the Dutch United Provinces! Portraits, indeed, were to be executed of huge proportions, sometimes of four-and-twenty life-size figures in one canvas, as we see in Van der Helst's great banquet scene ; but these great groups were ordered for the hospitals and town-halls, and not by the churches : and Dutch art was principally confined to small paintings for the small rooms of the merchants of Amsterdam and the Hague. Solomon and the Queen of Sheba, Samson and Delilah, Judith and Holofernes, all these old favourites of earlier Flemish painters gave place in freed Holland to the old cobbler and his spouse, the housewife and her child, the gallant and his lady love, and such domestic scenes. Rembrandt, indeed, would now and again paint pictures from Holy Writ, but in a manner that no artist had ever dared to do. He represented the Man of Sorrows, as one poor among the poorest, miserable among the wretchedest, as one, indeed, a sufferer and acquainted with grief. They are pictures full of the divine compassion that fills the principal figure with more divinity than all the glories of nimbuses and crowns in the works of the Italian schools could bestow; but Rembrandt's sacred paintings were not intended to decorate the walls of a church. Few indeed even of Rembrandt's pupils attempted to paint sacred subjects; they knew the national taste, and took their models from the life and the scenes around them. It is sufficient to recall the names of Terborch, of Bol, of the Van Ostades, and half-a-dozen others, to illustrate this.

With Rembrandt in Holland—as with Rubens in the Netherlands—passed away the greatness of his school; both left pupils and imitators in plenty, but none of these attained the excellence of their masters.

In Holland, with the greatness and independence of their country the Dutch painters had risen and flourished, and with its decline and decay they also declined and decayed. The art had been a national and a spontaneous growth, born with the independence and freedom of its native soil : when that independence had lessened and the freedom was diminished, the native art, like the foliage on the parent tree, suffered with its lack of health. This was the history of art in ancient Greece and in Italy. It repeated itself in Holland in the seventeenth century.

Surely such a history points a moral, and this is how we read it :—

No national art can exist without liberty and independence.

The more liberty (constitutional, not democratic) and independence there is in a country, the more will art flourish and expand.

R. G.

GERARD VAN HONTHORST.

Born 1590.—*Died* 1656.

I N the gallery at Stafford House there hangs a painting
in which the figures are the size of life ; it represents
a scene of tragic interest, and is so grand in feeling, and so
truly pathetic, that this picture, once seen, is not easily
forgotten.

Beside a table sits an old, bearded man, before him
stands a prisoner ; both figures are seen only in profile, and
but one candle placed on the table lights the two faces.
All is dark around the principal figures ; faces, only dimly
seen in the background, gaze in wonder and silence at
the old man, and at the one who with pinioned hands
looks down so patiently and wearily at the other. The
old man is the High Priest, Caiaphas ; the "visage" of
the other, "so marred more than any man and his form
more than the sons of men," the Saviour's.

From early childhood this painting had always deeply
impressed the writer, and when later in life he found how
inferior the other works of the painter of Our Saviour
before Caiaphas are, the disappointment was great. Let
us quote what an English and a French writer on
matters of art say with regard to this painting. First,

Mrs. Jameson, who writes of it, "The profound, the abandonment of resignation in the head and figure of the Redeemer, cannot be regarded without emotion;" and Charles Blanc, in his *Lives of the Dutch Painters*, says, " I shall never forget the extraordinary impression that this picture made on me; at first one can not distinguish the subjects of the painting; the principal figure, poorly clad in a white serge dress over a red shirt, appears at first sight to be but a common malefactor, brought up in the night to be questioned by the magistrate; the eye can not, owing to the vivid light of the candle and the darkness around, take in for some time the meaning of the work ; but soon the subject seems to stand out and disclose itself, the face of the accused seems impregnated with an ineffable gentleness and a sublime resignation, the divinity is present, the handcuffed prisoner is the Son of God." This painting of Gerard van Honthorst has also been praised by Sandrart, and it caused Lanzi to write of the artist that he was " *degno di rappresentare un decoro anche le sacre storie.*"

Gerard van Honthorst was born at Utrecht in 1590. He studied under Abraham Bloemaert, but he visited Italy when about twenty, and settled in Rome, where he soon became known from the surprising ability he showed in imitating the manner of Caravaggio. On first visiting the Vatican he is said to have been greatly struck by the effect of the three-fold light in Raphael's fresco of the Delivery of St. Peter —a triple light, partly from the torches, partly from the angel, and partly from the moon ; henceforth, tradition says, he resolved to distinguish his painting by similar effects, and he carried this fancy to such an extent that he earned for himself the nickname of "Gherardo delle

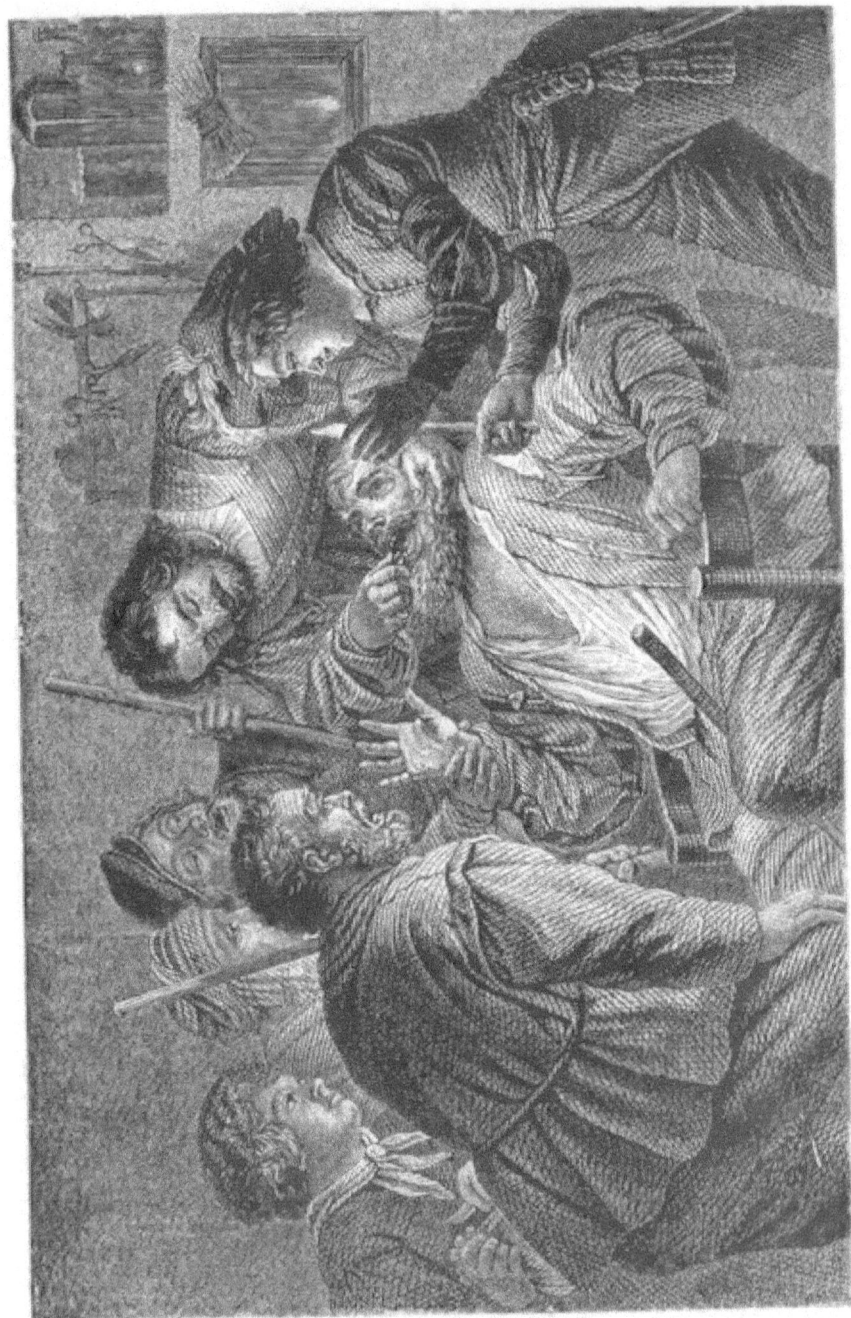

Notti."* It was during his stay in Rome that he painted the great picture already mentioned; it was done for his patron, Prince Giustiniani; he also executed many works of a religious character, and decorated the Church of Santa Maria della Scala with frescoes, one of which, representing the Martyrdom of St. John the Baptist, has been greatly admired.

On his return to Utrecht Honthorst was elected dean of the Guild of St. Luke in 1623; he then set up a school in which he taught many pupils; these appear to have been of a very aristocratic class, and, according to Horace Walpole, Honthorst had the "greatest honour" of giving lessons to the Queen of Bohemia and her children. One of these, Prince Rupert, did credit in after years to his master; probably it was through the Queen, his sister, that Charles I. heard of Honthorst. In 1628, the painter paid a visit of a few months to England, when Charles employed him to paint the Palace of Whitehall with allegorical subjects. Honthorst also while in this country painted several portraits; the best of these we believe to be that of the Countess of Bedford, at Woburn Abbey ; his group of the Duke and Duchess of Buckingham and their children, in the Royal Collection, is also very fine.

On his return to Holland, Honthorst decorated the Palace of the Hague; the House in the Wood; and Ryswick ; with his allegorical paintings, which, to judge from those we saw in the House in the Wood, were not of much merit. In 1636 he married Sophia Coopmans, and in the following year he was enrolled among the members of the Painters' Guild at the Hague; from 1645 to 1650 he received many commissions from Frederick Henry and William II., Princes of Orange.

* "Gerard of the Night."

Later in life Honthorst was employed by the King of Denmark, and many of his paintings are still to be seen in the palaces of Denmark.

Honthorst died at Utrecht on the 27th of April, 1656. Two of his sons followed in their father's profession : one of these, Willem Honthorst, was much in vogue as a portrait-painter ; he was employed by the Princess Louisa of Orange, who married the great Elector, and many of Willem Honthorst's portraits are in Berlin, whither he went in the train of that Princess in 1650.

The Louvre contains seven of Gerard Honthorst's works, but none of them are of first rate quality. There are many of his portraits in the Gallery at Amsterdam ; there are three in the Dresden Gallery ; and several in that of Munich ; and in the galleries of Florence, Berlin, and St. Petersburg, where there is a poor replica of the Stafford House picture. But in no place is there a larger collection of his portraits than in Lord Craven's country seat, Coombe Abbey. All of these are portraits of the House of Stuart, and were brought over to England by the Queen of Bohemia ; but nowhere has the writer seen any painting by this artist to compare to his Christ before Caiaphas at Stafford House.

For List of Honthorst's Principal Paintings — See Appendix.

ADRIAEN BROUWER.

Born about 1605—*Died* 1638.

THAT the works of an artist who seldom painted any scenes but such as he found in taverns and ale-houses, of drunken peasants fighting in their anger over their cards and dice; that such paintings as these and similar subjects should, during two centuries, have been esteemed among the treasures and rarities of the world of art, proves that the man who created them must have had extraordinary talent.

It seems a strange chance (when we remember how little is known regarding the lives of better painters and men among the Dutch artists than the subject of this sketch) that any details at all of the life of Adriaen Brouwer, the representative painter of brawls and drunken orgies, should be known. As told by Houbraken and Descamps, his life is indeed but a sad record of the career of a man gifted with genius which was wasted on most degrading objects; of a man so hopelessly wrong-minded and profligate that he preferred the company of boors and clowns to the society of the prince of painters; of one who almost literally threw his talents into the gutter—a career which ended in a hospital. But later researches have discovered sufficient to do more than throw doubt even on these statements; and in all probability Adriaen Brouwer was one of the many Dutch painters whose characters suffered much at the hands of their historians.

No one, we think, who looks at a fine etching of Van Dyck's, representing a handsome courtier, wearing his long love locks and upturned moustache, of refined features and a handsome person, with his cloak so negligently, but yet so gracefully, thrown across his shoulders— no one can believe that this attractive gallant was the boon-companion of the hideous bloat-faced rustics and drunken ruffians that he has immortalised in many an etching and painting, and with whom his days were said to have been passed.

Adriaen Brouwer * was born about the year 1605, probably at Oudenaerde.† His mother made dresses, and cut out patterns for these dresses, for the peasant women of Haarlem. He early showed his artistic bent when assisting his mother at her work, and drew the patterns and flowers with which she ornamented her clients' gowns.

One day, it is related, Frans Hals saw little Brouwer at this work : struck by his skill, he offered to make a painter of him, provided he was lodged, fed, and clothed by Hals. The mother of Brouwer had no objections to make to this proposition, and Adriaen went away with Hals, full of delight at the thoughts of at last becoming a painter. Poor little Brouwer was, however, to be cruelly disappointed. Hals was as avaricious as he was gifted, and his wife was avaricious without being gifted ; they worked the poor little fellow almost to death, and starved him into the bargain.

---

* It is sometimes written "de Brauwere" or "Brauwer"—but the way given above is the most correct.

† Haarlem is by some considered to be his birthplace.

Such at least is the account given by Houbraken, which Descamps colours still more vividly. He states that the child would have probably died of this cruel treatment had not some of Hals's pupils relieved him ; but at length Brouwer could stand his life with Hals no longer, and escaped, taking refuge in the cathedral, and hiding under the great organ, which Handel was to render so famous a century after the poor half-starved little painter had crouched under its massive pipes. Here he was discovered by a compassionate stranger, who engaged him to return to Hals's studio on the condition of his meeting with kinder treatment there. But not long did he remain there. Adriaan van Ostade persuaded him again to make his escape, and assured him that he had sufficient talent to earn a living without the assistance of others. Brouwer took this advice, and again decamped.

On this occasion he went further than the cathedral of Haarlem, not resting till he found himself in Amsterdam, where, at the sign of the "Ecu de France," he fell into good hands, the landlord and his son being both fond of art and artists. In a few days he had painted a picture, for which he was paid a hundred ducats ; these he lost no time in spending. Whenever he got any money, he spent it immediately in drink, and, as may be imagined, this system had its disadvantages.

It would be unnecessary to enter here into any further details of this artist's short and wasted life, as related by Descamps. Let it be sufficient to add that, having lost all he had gained at Amsterdam, he bethought himself of trying what success he might find at Antwerp ; but not having provided himself with a pass, he was arrested and thrown into prison as a spy.

Luckily for Brouwer, in the same prison the Duke of

Arenberg was also detained, on political grounds; to him Brouwer appealed, and the Duke, who was a good judge of a picture, having sent to Rubens for colours and brushes, got Brouwer to paint him one : the subject was all ready to be taken—a group of guards at their cards. Brouwer surpassed himself : the Duke was delighted with his fellow-captive's talent, and sent for Rubens, who, on seeing the work, exclaimed that no one but Brouwer could have painted the picture. That picture is still, we believe, in the Arenberg Gallery at Brussels.

Rubens having succeeded in getting Brouwer out of durance vile, invited him to his house ; but Sir Peter Paul led too stately and well-regulated a life for Adriaen Brouwer, who afterwards declared that he could not tell which was the worst to stay in, the prison or Rubens's palace.

We next hear of our artist teaching Van Craesbeeck how to paint ; making love at the same time to his pupil's wife. Existing documents show that in 1631 Brouwer was received into the Guild of St. Luke at Antwerp, and three years afterwards was made a member of the Society of Artists called "The Violet." These facts are strangely at variance with Descamps's account of this painter's vagabond life. Brouwer died at Antwerp in 1638, and was buried on the 1st of February in the church of the Carmelites.*

That both Rubens and Rembrandt thought highly of

---

* M. Van der Willigen discovered in the Mortuary Register of Haarlem, with the date 31st March, 1640, the following note :— " For opening a grave in the great church, for Adriaan Brouwer : the bells sounded half an hour, ƒ 8," which was then thought to refer to the painter's death ; but Dr. Wilhelm Schmidt has discovered that the " Schilder Brouwer" died towards the end of January, 1638, at Antwerp, and was buried by the Carmelites on the 1st of February. It is supposed that the second date has reference to the re-interment of the body by Rubens.

THE TOPERS.

By Adriaen Brouwer.

Brouwer's talent is shown by the fact that the former had seventeen of Brouwer's paintings, and the latter a similar number, and a large quantity of his drawings also. This artist's chief excellence was the harmony and brilliancy of his colours. His works are full of rich warm shadows and mellow half-tones. Owing to this charm of colour, and their rarity, Brouwer's paintings are as eagerly bought by wealthy amateurs as the works of Teniers or of Dou.

The Louvre has only one Brouwer. Our National Gallery has not a single specimen. The Hermitage at St. Petersburg but few; but there are Brouwers to be met with in the galleries of the Hague, at Amsterdam, and at Florence. By far the richest collection of Brouwers in any public gallery is that of Munich, which contains nine; six of these, Waagen tells us, are masterpieces. There is a beautiful little Brouwer at Dresden; one of his favourite scenes of a drunken quarrel between peasants. Sir Richard Wallace has a good example, and Lord Bute has two. The finest Brouwer we have seen in any private collection is one at Bridgewater House, a picture only ten inches high by seven broad; subject, a party of drunken peasants singing and shouting in a most uproarious manner. But uninviting as is the subject, and though ugly the actors, this little painting is as brilliant as a gem; and it is certainly one of the most valuable of the Dutch paintings contained in that noble collection. M. Bürger remarks that so rare are this painter's works in the art-markets of Europe, that Correggio's and Raphael's are oftener to be met with than Brouwer's.

For List of Brouwer's Principal Paintings—See Appendix.

GERARD TER-BORCH.

Born 1608—*Died* 1681.

IN his *Art Rambles in Belgium, Holland, and Italy,* Mr. F. W. Fairholt writes, "Imitative art can never be carried further than it was by Terborch in his famous picture known as The Satin Gown," a picture which has been made more celebrated by the notice it has received from Goethe in his *Wahlverwandtschaften.* He describes it as representing a noble, knightly-looking man, who sits with one leg over the other addressing himself to the conscience of his daughter, who stands before him. She is a majestic figure, in a full and flowing dress of white satin; her back only is seen, but the whole attitude shows that she is struggling with her feelings. The mother, too, seems to be concealing a little embarrassment, for she looks into a wine-glass out of which she is sipping. The extraordinary qualities it possesses as a transcript of nature are unrivalled, and the satin gown of the principal figure is reality itself.

With all due deference to the great German poet's description of Terborch's "satin-gown" picture, we cannot but think that he has magnified a very clever portrait group into a work of pathos, and coloured with his poetical sense a group in which the painter had only

THE LUTE-PLAYER.

BY GERARD TERBORCH.

In the Cassel Gallery.

wished to show his marvellous power of rendering the
quality and texture of a white satin gown on a grace-
ful female form, relieved by the black dress of another
lady and by the buff jerkin of a cavalier, who neither
appears old enough to be the father of the lady in the
satin gown, nor does his attitude or his expression convey
in the least the idea of correction.

It is in fact merely one of the many *genre* pictures (or
as the old art-books called them, *tableaux de modes*) which
the Mierises and the Metsus were wont to paint.

Gerard Ter Borch * was born at Zwolle in 1608. His
father, who had visited Italy, taught him how to paint.
He was then sent to Haarlem for further instruction, and
he visited Germany and Italy while still a youth. In
his early years he painted portraits on a small scale, with
great success. Happening to be at Münster in 1646, at
the time of the peace congress, and having made the
acquaintance of the Spanish minister, the Count de
Peñaranda, he was commissioned—probably by the latter
— to paint the extraordinary little picture representing
the scene, which, having successively passed through many
of the finest private collections in France, has, thanks
to the munificence of Sir Richard Wallace, found a final
resting-place in our National Gallery. This picture—
The Peace of Münster (No. 896)—is certainly of its kind
the most perfect that exists. Had Terborch painted
nothing else it would have rendered his name immortal in
the annals of art. It is painted on copper; and signed
G. T. BORCH.

Terborch visited the courts of Spain, France, and England. It is singular that neither in Spain nor England have

* Or " Terborch "—the common form " Terburg " is wrong.

any paintings been discovered that he executed during his stay in these countries.

In Spain Philip IV. received Terborch right royally, knighting him and loading him with gifts and honours.

What success he had in England is not known, nor the length of the stay he made in this country; even Horace Walpole is silent regarding these points.

What a treasure would it not be if one could discover the portrait of Cromwell painted by this artist !

It seems that Terborch soon tired of foreign courts and countries, and longed to return to his native country —Ower-Issel, which, according to Houbraken, was the pleasantest of all the United Provinces, and was then regarded as the Garden of Holland.

On Terborch's return to Holland he probably resided for a short time at Haarlem, for his name is mentioned in the records of the Guild of that town; he finally settled in Deventer, where he married one of his cousins, and became a member of the town council. In a little portrait by him-self in the Hague Museum, we see the artist in his costume of "regent," or town councillor, not, as Bürger says, in that of a burgomaster, for Terborch never attained to that elevation in the rank of citizenship.

He wears a most majestic wig, the curls of which shade a long and somewhat melancholy visage ; over his shoulder is flung a dark cloak, which falls as far as the knees in heavy folds; black knots are tied below the knees, beneath the long grey stockings; he wears high-heeled shoes, square-toed, with large black rosettes on the instep, such as we see worn by Molière's characters at the Comédie Française.

Although this portrait is but two feet high by one foot five inches across, one feels that were one to meet this

PATERNAL ADVICE.   BY GERARD TERBORCH.

In the Amsterdam Museum.

individual in the street, he would be recognised as the
painter immediately : the face, as we have already said, is
a somewhat sad one; the nose well shaped and long; a
firm mouth is shaded with a moustache already grey, for
when the painter stood for this picture he was fifty years
of age. The date is about 1660.

As Bürger remarks, he often introduces into his *genre*
pictures individuals like himself. Terborch had the honour
of portraying William III.'s harsh features, harsh already,
although he was then only two-and twenty, on the occasion
of that Prince's visiting Deventer in 1672.

William is reported to have barely given Terborch time
to paint more than a sketch; but this was considered such
a wonderful likeness, that an amateur at Amsterdam got
it in exchange for a coach. We do not know what has
become of this most interesting work. What a precious
addition it would be were our National Portrait Gallery
able to obtain it !

It appears that our artist lived on quietly at Deventer
till his death, which occurred in 1681 ; he had then
attained the respectable age of seventy-three. He left no
children.

Terborch's pictures are among the great rarities of
Continental and English Galleries. Only eighty of his
pictures have been classified. Of these, four are at the
Louvre; the finest of these is a picture of an officer offering a handful of money to a lady who is seated at a
table laden with fruit, the inevitable wine-glass in her
hand.

Of this painting Kugler writes :—"The animation of
the heads, the drawing, the finely-balanced silvery tone,
and the equally careful and fine treatment, render this a
chef-d'œuvre of the master."

At Amsterdam, in the Museum, are portraits of himself and his wife ; and a fine group of a boy and a dog in the Van der Hoop Gallery ; there were two in the Van Loon Collection.*

In the Museum at the Hague are two ; one of these is the painter's portrait, the other the famous Trumpeter ; this Kugler thinks "especially admirable for the fine chiaroscuro and the delicate harmony of the broken colours."

In the Berlin Museum are eight Terborchs ; one of these is the famous "satin gown" picture—Paternal Advice, a work of which there are many repetitions ; one of the best of these is in the Bridgewater Gallery, and is a better specimen than either the one at Berlin or that at Amsterdam.

At the Gallery at Cassel are two good examples—one a lady playing on a lute. This is a charming little picture ; the face is prettier than Terborch usually painted, and the satin gown has all the marvellous sheen and brilliancy in which Terborch has never been rivalled, with perhaps the one exception of Millais's lady in the Black Brunswicker.

The Dresden Gallery has four Terborchs ; the best of them are a lady—of course in white satin—washing her hands in a silver basin, and an officer writing a letter for which a trumpeter is in waiting. There are good specimens at Munich, Lyons, Montpellier, and at Florence, as is generally the case with the Dutch school. In the Hermitage Gallery at St. Petersburg, Terborch is richly represented by half-a-dozen fine examples.

Our National Gallery contains, besides the matchless little (small in size but great in treatment) picture of the Peace

* This valuable collection is now dispersed.

of Münster, recently mentioned, a charming little work called the Guitar Lesson, for which the late Sir Robert Peel gave 920 guineas.

Terborch had a sister, Gezina, who was an excellent copyist of her brother's works; many of her copies, according to Smith, having been retouched by Terborch, have since passed for original works.

Among the most distinguished of Terborch's pupils and imitators may be mentioned Caspar Netscher, Metsu, and G. van den Eeckhout, born in 1621 at Amsterdam, some of whose pictures, generally of soldiers gambling, are almost as fine as Terborch's.

We know one at Stafford House which, were it not for its somewhat too brown tone and dark shadows, might easily be taken for a Terborch, so clever is the grouping and so masterly the workmanship.

ADRIAAN JANSZ, VAN OSTADE.

Born 1610.—Died 1685.

A T the beginning of the seventeenth century there was
settled at Haarlem one Jan Hendricx, who, driven
away possibly by the fear of military strife and religious
persecutions, had come from the town of Eyndhoven, a
neighbourhood famous for the production of cloth; he
was in all probability a weaver. Early in 1605 we find him
settled at Haarlem, and married to Janneke Hendericdr,*
of Wonsel,† a village near Eyndhoven. The marriage was
a fruitful one; they had eight children—four girls and
four boys—whom they were able to bring up in ease, if
not in luxury. Their eldest child, Marijte, married Barent
Bosvelt, of Warendorp (a village near Münster), who was
Secretary of Haarlem.

In 1610 their eldest son—the third child—was born,
and on the 10th of December of the same year he was
baptized, receiving the name of Adriaan. This was
Adriaan van Ostade! The sobriquet, Van Ostade, was
adopted by the children at various times in their several
careers. We do not find it mentioned in connection with
Adriaan Jansz until 1636, in which year he is recorded as
a member of the Civic Guard, in the company known as
the "Oude Schuts." The name, Ostade, was derived from

* Daughter of Henry.   † *i.e.* Woensel.

a small hamlet of that name,* probably the birth-place
of their father, near Eyndhoven. As Adriaan signed
himself Van Ostade † on almost all his works, it has, not
unnaturally, been looked upon as a surname.

Adriaan left to his brother Johannes the trade of weav-
ing, while he and the youngest child, Isack, adopted the
profession of art. He entered the studio of Frans Hals,
and was there a fellow student of Adriaen Brouwer. On
the completion of his apprenticeship he set up as a painter
in his native town, and there he lived in good circumstances, laboured with industry, and died respected. In
1638 he married Machtelgen Pietersen, a young lady, a
native of Haarlem; but fate did not permit him to enjoy
many years of unalloyed happiness. Sorrows fell fast upon
him. In 1640 his mother died; in the following year he
lost his father; and in 1642 his young wife was taken
from him, after a short wedded life of but little more than
four years. That he married again has been ascertained,
though history is silent as regards the name of his second
choice. Again he was left a widower, in 1666.

On the 27th of April, 1685, in the Nieuwe Kruysstraet,
Adriaan Jansz died; and on the 2nd of May he was
buried in the Church of St. Bavon, where he had previously
laid the remains of his two wives.

In the June of the same year a sale took place of the
works of art left at his death—they included, besides the
paintings of other masters, two hundred pictures by his
own hand, his etchings, drawings, &c. His son-in-law,
Dirk van der Stoel, surgeon of Haarlem—the husband of
his only child Johanna Maria—appears to have bought the
etchings, for in the July he held a sale of them.

* Now called Ostedt.
† He occasionally, in early life, signed " Ostaden."

ADRIAAN VAN OSTADE.
FROM A PAINTING BY HIMSELF.

Until the researches of M. van der Willegen brought to light many details concerning the life of Van Ostade, much misinformation had been written, from Houbraken downwards. He was wrongly called a native of Lübeck, and it was stated, without sufficient foundation, that he painted much at Amsterdam, and that he died there.

Van Ostade has left a name which—although he seldom painted subjects more ambitious than peasants and scenes from out "the short and simple annals of the poor "—is among the most distinguished of the Dutch figure painters.

That able French art critic whom we have quoted more than once in these sketches, says happily of Adriaan van Ostade, that he is a kind of "Rembrandt in little."

Certainly he approaches nearer to the great masters, as a colourist, than even Gerard Dou himself, and also in the management of his transparent shadows; occasionally even he produces in his pictures those deep golden tones for which Rembrandt is celebrated, and his power of grouping his figures is also Rembrandtesque.

Adriaan worked at a period when the Dutch school had reached its zenith, when Gerard Dou was making those wondrous gems which have been the envy and despair of his imitators, when Wouwerman and Lingelbach were producing charming hunting scenes and hawking parties, when Paulus Potter was giving more life to his horses and cattle than any artist had till that day attempted, and which no animal painter equalled until Edwin Landseer came; and high above all these lesser lights blazed the prodigious genius of the son of the Leyden miller, the greatest master of light and shadow that the world of art has produced.

The affinity between some of Van Ostade's interiors and those of Rembrandt have not unnaturally made writers on

Dutch art suppose that Adriaan worked among the Great Master's pupils. This, however, was not the case.

Van Ostade certainly caught somewhat of the magic power; some of the splendid colouring of Rembrandt. In many of Van Ostade's interiors the lights and shadows are as subtly managed as even in those of Rembrandt; look, for instance, at a picture of the old hall in which Van Ostade has shown us himself at work before his easel; how the darkness of this cloistered apartment can be felt; only one window admits the light through its narrow panes of glass, to fall brokenly in a hundred chequers on the old stone floor; in the dim distance beneath the winding staircase an apprentice is grinding the artist's colours. Is not Rembrandt's influence strongly marked in such a work?

Or look again at the interior of this old barn, in which peasants are carousing. Was ever such a common old building made to glow with light and shade as this does, and is it not almost worthy of Rembrandt's brush?

M. Charles Blanc, in his *Lives of the Dutch Painters*, has noticed that although Van Ostade—owing probably to the taste of his patrons more than to his own inclination— nearly always painted scenes of ruffianism and drunkenness, of boors fighting over their cups, etc., his own life was essentially a gentle and a decent one; in this respect he resembles Teniers.

To judge by the portrait he has left us of himself, painted when in middle life, he resembled rather a Covenanting preacher or a Methodist parson than the painter of brawls and junketings. He wears his hair long, falling over a plain deep collar: and his countenance is more grave than gay.

Of Van Ostade's pictures Smith gives a list of nearly four hundred; besides this great number of oil paintings,

THE HUNCHBACK FIDDLER.

By Adriaan van Ostade.

he executed an unknown number of water-colour paintings, as well as a vast quantity of pencil-drawings and etchings; of the latter, Bartsch has made a list of fifty. A fine collection of them is in the Teyler Museum, at Haarlem. These are much appreciated by collectors, and in their department are as excellent as his paintings, full of character and cleverness.

Of these etchings, mostly scenes of peasant life, studied among the lanes and villages in the neighbourhood of Haarlem, Mr. Hamerton, in his *Etching and Etchers*, writes:—"Early states of Van Ostade's etchings are now of great value, and have risen much in the market during the last twenty years. In 1838, Mr. Wilson's set was sold for 105*l*. Mr. Seguier afterwards gave 159*l*. 15*s*. for the same set, which eventually fetched 500*l*. It is now worth a thousand guineas, ten times its value twenty years ago!"

Of Van Ostade's paintings the Louvre possesses seven fine examples; among the best of which is the one where the painter has represented himself surrounded by his family. In the Munich Gallery are also fine Van Ostades; and there are six in the Gallery at Dresden. The Hermitage, St. Petersburg, is particularly rich in his works, containing no less than twenty. Our National Gallery has but one; there are four in the Amsterdam Gallery, including the well-known Baker blowing a Horn, and two in the Hague Museum, besides some in the Six Collection.

The public galleries of Antwerp, Brussels, and Madrid contain works by Adriaan; and in the Bridgewater House Gallery are some fine examples of this master. Two are especially good; both represent an old man—probably a lawyer—in whom Van Ostade seems to have had a special delight as a model. There are also paintings by Van Ostade in the Royal Collection and in Lord Bute's Gallery.

Besides his younger brother Isack, Adriaan had the following pupils:—Dusart, Cornelis Bega, Michiel van Musscher, Richard Brakenburgh, and Jan Steen; these all closely imitated Adriaan's manner, and of them his brother Isack was the most talented.

It is worthy of remark that in his early manner Adriaan van Ostade, while under the influence of his master Hals, had more dash and bravura in his style of painting, which latterly became more laboured and more elaborately finished; but he never degenerated into the "tea-tray" painting of Mieris or Metsu.

FERDINAND BOL.

Born 1611—*Died* 1681.

THE earliest and best of Rembrandt's many pupils was undoubtedly Ferdinand Bol. Of his life we know little. He was born at Dordrecht in 1611; went when a child with his parents to Amsterdam, his future home; studied under Rembrandt; was made a citizen; married, in 1653, Elisabeth Dell; and died there in 1681.

In the town-hall of Amsterdam hangs a large painting representing, on a canvas eight feet long by six high, the Burgomaster of the town, seated with three other "Regents" or Governors of the Lepers' hospital. The maintenance of this institution was finally done away with in 1862; and the paintings were then removed from the building to the town-hall; and among them went Bol's Four Regents. These worthy and reverend signiors are clad in black, and wear large broad-brimmed hats; the solemnity of their garb is relieved by the rich Persian covering of the table round which they are grouped; they appear as distinguished as any of Van Dyck's sitters, and are as solidly painted as any of Rembrandt's portraits. An attendant leads in a poor child whose disfigured head tells the story and motive of the work.

Charles Blanc mentions that on the occasion of an
exhibition of paintings for some charitable purpose, this
painting, which had been hung, almost forgotten and
unnoticed, for two centuries in the old Leper House, created
quite a sensation; and that during the exhibition Rembrandt was neglected for the sake of this fine work by
his pupil.

A PHILOSOPHER IN MEDITATION. By FERDINAND BOL.

Another life-size group of portraits, which was formerly
in the same building, representing the lady patronesses of
the establishment, is equally fine; and as Bürger remarks,
when one has seen these two works, one places Bol above
Van der Helst himself, and only second to Rembrandt.

However, to our thinking, Bol was a most uncertain

painter, and, although, while under the influence of Rembrandt, he produced works that may have passed as being the work of the master himself, he latterly degenerated into a bad imitator of Rembrandt, and appears even to have exaggerated the faults of his manner and style without retaining the power of giving the superb effects of light and shade which, while in that master's studio, he certainly once possessed. This change is apparent in those paintings of Bol that bear a later date than 1660, when he had probably left Rembrandt. With Flinck, he loses himself completely in attempting to affect the Italian style of art, and in his allegorical paintings he seems even to caricature the faults of his great master.

After the great geniuses come the little ones ; after the great masters, the small painters ; such has been the case in all the Italian, Flemish, and Dutch schools. After the glory of Raphael and Michelangelo, the decadence of the Italian school rapidly approached ; and as it was in Italy, so it was to be in Flanders and in Holland—the sun once set, darkness spread over the world of art.

Ferdinand Bol has left a score of etchings of scriptural and other subjects, which are much sought after by collectors. The principal of these are Abraham's Sacrifice ; Sacrifice of Gideon ; Saint Jerome in his Cave ; The Astrologer ; A Philosopher in Meditation ; An Old Man with a curled Beard ; The Woman with a Pear ; An Old Man's Head in an oval (this is an extremely rare etching, and, according to C. Blanc, is as fine as any of Rembrandt's), and The Hour of Death, which Bartsch has placed among the etchings of Rembrandt.

In the Louvre are four paintings by Bol—two of these are portraits, the others imaginary subjects. At the Museum of the Hague are three fine portraits . by Bol, one

that of Admiral de Ruijter, and at Amsterdam there is
another of the Admiral, besides a fine portrait of the
sculptor, Arthur Quellinus.

The Berlin Gallery has a fine example of this painter,
and there are also two at Munich; but the galleries
wealthiest in his works are those of Dresden, where there
are three superb specimens; and St. Petersburg, which
contains ten fine portraits. In our National Gallery there
is a picture by him, called the Astronomer. In Lord
Northbrook's collection are a fine pair of portraits of a
man and his wife by Ferdinand Bol.

BARTHOLOMEUS VAN DER HELST.

Born 1613 (?)—*Died* 1670.

THERE is no one who, however little he may have
studied the Dutch school of painting, has not heard of
Paulus Potter's famous life-size figure of a Bull, of Rembrandt's School of Anatomy, or of his so-called Night Watch;
nor, having heard of these, is it likely that the fame of Van
der Helst's great banqueting scene has not reached him.

"Perhaps," writes Sir Joshua Reynolds of this great
group of portraits, "perhaps this is the first picture of
portraits in the world." How Sir Joshua could have made
his statement after having seen Rembrandt's Syndics, his
Dr. Tulp and pupils, and above all the Night Watch, is
not within our comprehension. We may here quote what
we wrote, soon after seeing this great group of portraits
in the Trippenhuis, at Amsterdam, in the same room
with Rembrandt's masterpiece : "You have but to turn
your back on the Night Watch to see before you another of
Holland's most renowned historical paintings, the *chef
l'œuvre* of Bartholomeus van der Helst, his *Schutters-
maaltijd*, the banquet given by the arquebusiers of this
town to celebrate the peace of Westphalia and the end of
the long war between their country and Spain. All the
world has seen prints and photographs of this work, and
to judge by their number it is a more popular picture than

the one by Rembrandt that hangs opposite. Art critics
have fought over the comparative merits of it and of The
Night Watch, not that there is any comparison necessary
or possible between such entirely different works, the one
being only a very splendidly painted group of portraits
which, though executed with extreme care and minuteness,
has several faults and weaknesses—for instance, the want
of any shadow, or consequent depth—while the other is
filled with a life and light of its own. . . . Every
detail of this banqueting scene is most carefully finished,
down to the lemon-rinds and knives on the table—forks
were apparently not used, except by the carver, in Van der
Helst's time. The fault of this picture seems to be its
total want of repose : the heads are quite bewildering, and
one cannot fix one's attention on any individual face ; the
eye runs along the row nearest to the spectator, and then
follows the line of heads on the further side of the table.
Many of the heads are full of expression and life, especially
that of stout old Banning, sitting with crossed legs, and a
blue banner in his hand." We have entered into some
length of description respecting this remarkable group of
twenty-four portraits, it being undoubtedly one of the
most famous works of the kind in existence ; painted
when the artist was but five-and-thirty, it shows that he
had early attained the highest place in his profession.

We find hardly anything regarding this painter's
career, and what we do find is of uncertain report.
He was probably the son of Severinus van der Helst
and Aaltje Hendricx, of Grave, and was born, it is
thought, in 1613, at Haarlem, where he passed his youth.
He is supposed to have studied under Pinas ; and Frans
Hals has also been suggested as his instructor in art.
By 1636 we find him settled at Amsterdam, and he was

par excellence the fashionable portrait painter of the day, and, strange as it now seems, he received much larger sums for his paintings than Rembrandt did for his. In the museum at Rotterdam is a picture painted by Van der Helst in 1656, representing a life-size group of a gentleman, his wife, and two children, for which he received 2,000 florins; it has been ascertained that whereas Rembrandt was glad to part with works for thirty and forty florins apiece—and we know that at the sale of his effects, forty of his pictures were sold for less than five thousand florins—Van der Helst never had less than 100 ducats for a half-length portrait. Sandrart tells us that Van der Helst married, in advanced life, Constantia Reijnst, of an ancient family of Amsterdam, and left one son, Lodewijk, who, Houbraken says, followed his father's profession.

Bartholomeus van der Helst died at Amsterdam in the year 1670, and was buried on the 10th of December, in the Walloon Church. Among an immense number of portraits he has left one of himself, in which he appears as a grand-looking man of fifty, lolling back in his chair and holding a miniature in his hand. Naturally, little individual interest attaches to Van der Helst's large corporation pictures, and we would prefer, had we the choice, the single portrait by him of Paulus Potter, said to have been taken three days before that artist's death, now in the museum at the Hague; a most pathetic and interesting little picture, and more to be desired than all the huge canvases at the Trippenhuis.

In the Six van Hillegrom collection a Amsterdam, are a couple of beautiful little portraits of the painter and his wife; they are miniatures in size and are as full of life as the largest of his portraits. In the Town Hall at

F P II   D

Amsterdam is an immense painting by Van der Helst in which thirty life-size portraits are painted with great power; it seemed to us to be worthy to form a pendant to his banqueting picture in the Trippenhuis; this fine work was, when we saw it, miserably hung in a narrow room and in a bad light.

The galleries and museums of Holland are full of this great portrait painter's works.   At the Louvre is a superb little group of figures: there are also examples in the galleries of Munich, Brussels, and St. Petersburg, and in our National Gallery is a fine portrait of a lady.

No one who saw the superb half-length of a Dutch Gentleman, dressed in black, exhibited in the Winter Exhibition of Old Masters, at Burlington House, in 1879, belonging to M. de Zoete (No. 68), will withhold from Van der Helst the right to rank among the great portrait painters of the seventeenth century.

GERARD DOU.

Born 1613—*Died* 1675.

DESCAMPS, who, in his Biographies of the Flemish, German, and Dutch painters, has saved from oblivion so much matter of interest concerning their lives, and who, with Houbraken, has done for them the same office that Vasari did for the Italian artists, tells us all that is recorded of the life of the greatest of the "Little Masters" of the Dutch School, Gerard * Dou.†

If taking infinite pains is a proof of genius, Gerard Dou was a true genius; it is recorded of this patient painter that he bestowed the labour of five days on the hand of a lady—a finger a day! that he passed more than three days of toil in copying a broom-stick, and that although he commenced painting when only fifteen years old, and worked incessantly until his death, at the age of sixty-two, only two hundred pictures of his are known in the various public and private galleries of Europe.

He was born at Leyden in 1613, in the same year and the same town which had the glory of claiming Rembrandt as citizen; and his father, Douwe Janszoon de Vries van Arentsvelt, who was a glazier, sensibly allowed his son to

---

* Or Gerrit, or Gerhard. † The form Dov is wrong.

follow the path to which the boy's instincts led him, and
apprenticed him, in 1622, to the studio of the engraver,
Bartholomeus Dolendo. Here young Gerard spent some
time in mastering the art of drawing. After quitting the
engraver's desk he entered, in 1624, the studio of Pieter
Kouwenhoven, a painter on glass. In a couple of years
young Dou was a better artist than his master, and his
father, delighted with his son's talent and rising reputation, and fearing to risk his life by allowing him to
mend windows and repair stained glass in the churches,
placed him, in 1628, in the studio of the great Rembrandt
van Rijn.

That an artist gifted as was Dou should have borrowed
so little of his master's style and manner, proves that he
had strong individuality; indeed it is difficult to understand how any painter, studying with, and under the eye
of, Rembrandt, could have had so little of that great
master's influence forced upon him. But Dou's talent
was all his own; his pictures, though small, are superb
specimens of the art of finish and care, and of what is of
still greater consequence, truth to nature.

After setting up for himself, Dou is reported to have
worked at portrait painting; but his manner was too slow
and laboured to please his sitters, and he soon saw that
success in this line was not to be obtained in representing
the Mynheers and Fraus of the Hague; but in immortalis-
ing traits of domestic life, in painting the scenes of humble
industry that the neighbouring Market Place contained,
and the interiors graced by buxom maids of his own or
neighbours' homes.

No details have been handed down to us of Dou's life.
It was probably passed happily and quietly at his beloved
work. He resided—with the exception of two gaps, of from

1651 to 1657, and again from 1668 to 1672—in his native city. That he was a prosperous gentleman is to be inferred from the large sums for which he sold his paintings. The wealthy connoiseur Van Spiring gave Dou an annual donation of a thousand florins merely to be allowed to have the first choice of the pictures that the artist had completed at the close of every year. Besides this annual grant, Van Spiring paid the ordinary price of the pictures he chose, like any other purchaser.

Gerard Dou died at Leyden in 1675, and was buried in the Church of St. Peter on the 9th of February.

It is recorded that when Charles II. returned to England the States-General could think of no more precious gift to present to His Majesty than one of Dou's works, and this is said to have been one of his beautiful little interiors, in which a mother is nursing her child. Some chroniclers say this painting was not presented to the King by the States-General, but by the Directors of the Dutch East Indian Company. The price of the work is said to have been 4,000 florins.

Dou ruined his sight by the minute finish of his painting, and was consequently obliged to wear glasses when only thirty years old. Descamps gives an exact description of an instrument in which a diminishing-glass was placed which enabled Dou to see what he was copying on the same scale as the picture on which he was at work.

The privileged few he admitted to his studio did not fail to notice the precautions he took to prevent a particle of dust from settling on his brushes or his canvas; so far did he carry this precaution, that his studio was protected as much as possible from that earthy element by a large ditch filled with water. He mixed his own colours and made his own brushes, and prepared the varnishes which

have preserved his exquisite little paintings with such
wonderful freshness for hundreds of years after the
careful hands that executed them had returned to that
dust which he so much dreaded. |

Dou delighted in painting his own portraits, in which
he appears a bright-eyed, frank, and intelligent-looking
man. There are two of these works in the gallery at
Bridgewater House; in one of these, perhaps the most
perfect of Dou's pictures in the world, we see him sitting
in his studio: he has taken up his fiddle, and laid aside
his brushes; his costume rather affects the cavalier, for
he is booted and spurred, and wears his velvet cap,
with its jaunty feather, on one side of his comely head;
but the surroundings proclaim the artist and the student,
although a riding cloak and a rapier are slung on the
wall; a folio volume lies spread open on the green baize
table, and a globe of the world stands behind; in a niche
beneath the spiral staircase beyond is another globe,
probably that of the heavens; while the empty flagon on
the floor, and the, doubtless not entirely unfilled, barrel of
beer looks as if the painter thoroughly appreciated the
good things of this life.

Holland is still rich in Dou's works. In the Gallery at
Amsterdam is one of his most celebrated performances.
This represents a school at night; unfortunately it has
much darkened by age.

Another of his well-known works is that called the
Femme Hydropique, which is one of the treasures in the
salon carré of the Louvre. This painting has also somewhat darkened. Another, said to have been as good, went
down with the ship which sank, laden with rare paintings,
when on its way to St. Petersburg, in the reign of the
Empress Catherine II.

However, St. Petersburg, in the Gallery of the Hermitage, can boast of a very fine show of Dou's paintings. It contains no less than twelve. (See Appendix, page 97.) The Gallery at Dresden is also one of the richest as regards Dou's works. In our National Gallery are three examples: there are also some fine specimens in the private galleries of England; but none more charming than those already alluded to at Bridgewater House. There is a fine Dou at Grosvenor House. We cannot but think that Sir Joshua Reynolds was rather hard in his criticism on Dou when he said of his paintings, that one looks at them " with admiration on the lips, and indifference in the heart." That a little picture no bigger than the palm of one's hand does not make the pulse beat faster, as the creation of a Titian or a Rembrandt may do, is doubtless true ; but that the perfection of finish and the beauty of workmanship in Dou's paintings are a delight to the eye and a pleasure to the mind, is unquestionable.

Gerard Dou was not only in his special line of art a consummate master, but he formed other painters, several of whom, although they did not attain to his extraordinary skill of finish, left many fine works to posterity. Among these followers, Frans van Mieris holds a foremost place. But mention must also be made of Godfried Schalcken, Gabriel Metsu, and Pieter Cornelisz van Slingeland.

Another proof of Dou's talent as a painter is, that the engravings of his pictures are remarkable for the subtle beauty of their light and shade, and have been among the finest works in black and white with which the Dutch school has enriched the world of engraving.

PHILIPS WOUWERMAN.

Born 1619—*Died* 1668.

OF Philips Wouwerman, Sir Joshua Reynolds says, "He is one of the few painters whose excellence in his particular department is such as leaves us nothing to wish for."

But what is Wouwerman's "particular department"? Is it in figure-painting, or as an animal painter, or as a landscape-artist that his excellence is so great?

We would answer, in all three departments—for Wouwerman was one of those very rare geniuses who painted figures, animals, and landscapes with equal facility, a combination of talent as extraordinary as it is rare.

There is a superb collection of engravings from this gifted artist's works; a large folio of some hundred plates, in which, although the subjects are similar, there is no repetition in any. In this work, which might be called Wouwerman's *Liber Studiorum*, the wonderful talent and variety of the artist are better seen than in any gallery in which his paintings appear.

We know very little of Wouwerman's * life. He was the son of Paulus Joosten Wouwerman, of Alkmaar, and

* Wouverman, Wouwermans, and other forms, are also found in the biographies of this painter.

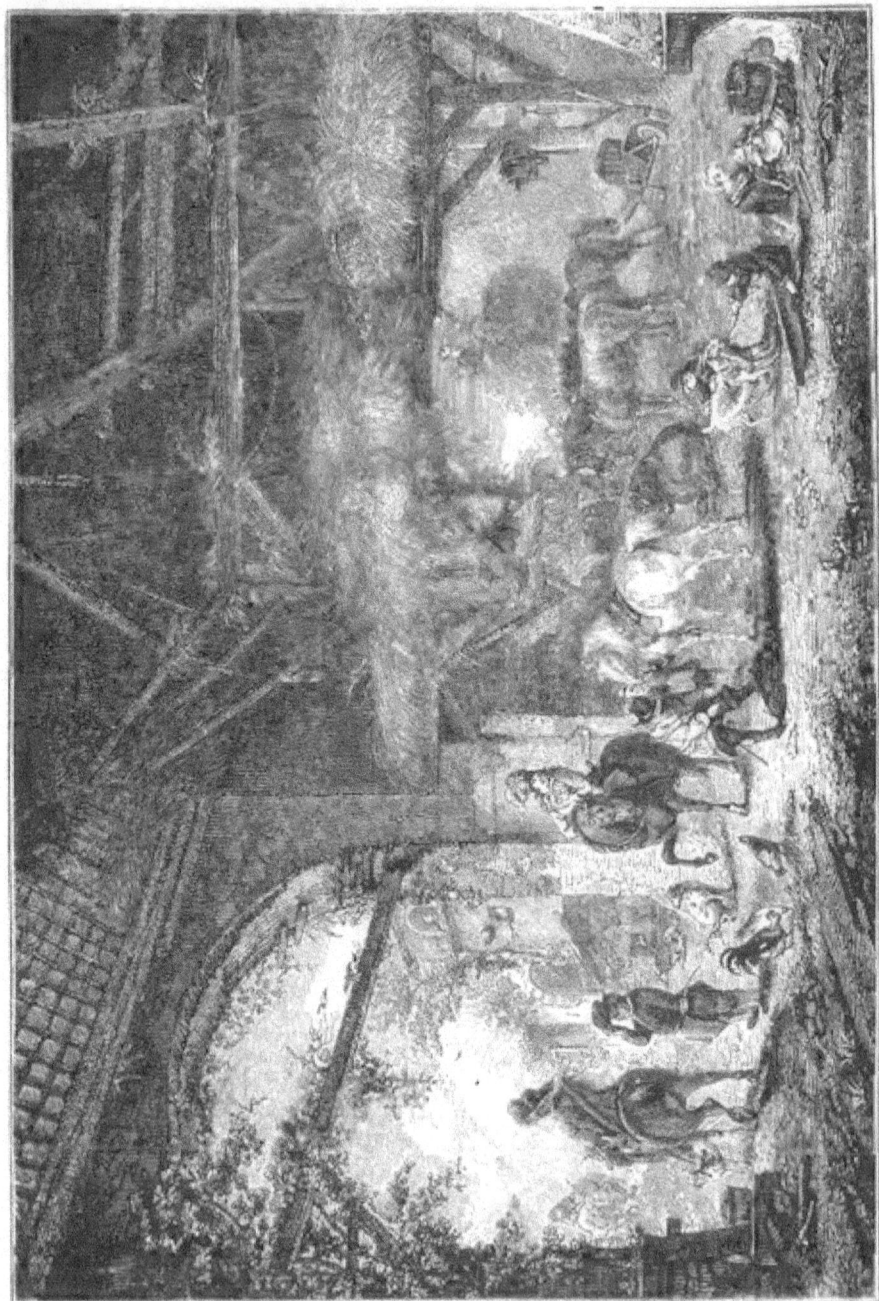

Susanneke van den Bogaert, of Croft, his third wife. Philips was born at Haarlem in 1619, and was baptized on the 24th of May. He first studied under his father, who was a second-rate historical painter. Later on, he worked in Wijnant's studio. At the age of nineteen he made a run-away marriage at Hamburg, where he studied a short time under Evert Decker. He returned, however, to Haarlem, where he entered the Guild in 1640, and where he lived in comfortable circumstances.

He died in 1668, at the early age of forty-nine, and was buried in the New Church on the 23rd of May—the day before the anniversary of his birthday. He left a larger number of works than any of his contemporary fellow artists; paintings in which it is not easy to know which most to admire, whether the beauty of their composition and grouping, the brilliancy and clear tone of their colouring, or their wonderful variety.

What a charm there is even in the name of Philips Wouwerman! It brings before the mind's eye pictures and scenes of the brightest and most animated kind; of cavaliers and their dames hunting the deer or hawking the heron; cantering across the pleasant sunny fields, under the shadowy woods, and adown the cool glens; or pacing slowly by the reedy ponds or sedgy streams. Of halts of cavalry beneath gay pavilions, and tents spread below the leafy branches of ancient oaks and hoary elms; of wild charges and forays in which the fiery Rupert would have felt at home; here and there the smoke has cleared, showing the varied fortunes of the fight; a dozen pistols are levelled towards that pennon that still remains the centre of the combat; riderless horses plunge madly away, and one feels as if one heard all the wild turmoil of the hand-to-hand encounter. Or, again, in another and more peaceful scene, we enter with some troopers the vast barn which they have converted into a stable. Or, again, a view opens full of pomp and of pleasure : it is a wide landscape, in the foreground a palace with terraces and fountains, beyond, a luxurious champaign. The furthest distance, bounded by a range of soft blue mountains; on the terraced slopes, ladies in splendid dresses animate the scene, attended by pages who bear aloft huge parasols ; in the courtyard below, a gay cavalcade is preparing to join another mounted party that is winding down the avenue ; thirsty dogs are quenching their thirst in the marble fountains, and a huntsman is blowing his bugle to collect the stragglers of the pack.

Where could the Haarlem painter have seen such fairy scenes and palaces?—not in Holland. This must have been an artist's dream, perhaps a vision of a castle in Spain.

In another picture we are transported from the sparkling skies and castled slopes; the scene is less gay, the sky less bright, and here the tragic predominates ; a gloomy path, half lost in the skirts of a dark forest, out of which a heavily-laden wagon has crept, dragged by four wretched-looking cart-horses, ridden by panic-stricken peasants. A sudden attack by banditti has caused this unpleasant surprise, and, to judge by the number and appearance of the highwaymen, these poor peasants would fare badly were it not that two mounted cavaliers, who seem well armed, are gallantly riding up to the rescue. These, and a hundred similar scenes—similar, but always differently treated—are recalled when the name of Philips Wouwerman is spoken ; whether he painted pictures gay or sad, of peace or war, he always painted as if his whole heart and mind were in his work. Every picture that we know by him is a complete, and often a perfect, work in itself. Out of the prodigious number, Smith, in his *Catalogue Raisonné*, has enumerated over seven hundred. Wouwerman's pictures never repeat themselves, nor are his favourite white horse, or sorrel mare, his dappled grey, or strawberry-roan, the same in any two of his paintings. Never surely was a painter who confined himself to similar subjects so infinitely varied. As is often the case in artistic biographies where little is known regarding a painter of such celebrity as Philips Wouwerman, foolish tales and worthless anecdotes are repeated concerning them in order to help the writer to fill up space. Not content with the certain but very meagre facts we know regarding Wouwerman, a legend has been repeated, even by the most recent of his biographers, to the effect that he destroyed all his studies and sketches shortly before his death in order that his brothers and son—who were also artists—should not make money by them. We cannot believe that Philips Wouwerman had so sordid a mind.

Connoisseurs pretend that they can detect three different styles or manners in this painter's works : the first, rather foxy in colour and awkward in drawing ; the second, less so ; and the third, of that silvery grey tone of colour which lends so much charm to the artist's simplest scenes, and to his plainest landscapes.

Wouwerman sometimes, but very rarely, painted Scriptural subjects ; two such are in the Gallery at Dresden : one represents the Annunciation to the Shepherds, the other St. John the Baptist Preaching in the Wilderness. They are both refined in treatment and beautiful in execution, but one certainly prefers the unscriptural works, in which he is more at home. It is impossible that all, or even a large portion of the paintings that pass as original works by Wouwerman can be from that master's hand.

The Dresden Gallery alone contains a number of works sufficient to have engrossed half his lifetime; there are almost as many at St. Petersburg, in the Gallery of the Hermitage; at Munich there are seventeen; in the galleries of his native land Wouwerman is also very largely represented. At the Louvre are at least half-a-dozen good examples, and seven are in our National Gallery. In Buckingham Palace are ten of his pictures, of which the one known as the *Coup de Pistolet* is one of his finest works. We cannot do more here than allude to those private collections in this country in which this delightful painter's works are conspicuous. The Bridgewater Gallery has some fine specimens, so has Grosvenor House; Lords Ashburton, Overstone, and Feversham and Sir Richard Wallace possess good examples, as well as Mr. Morrison, Mr. Walter, and many others.

Both Wouwerman's brothers, Pieter and Jan, painted similar subjects. Of these brothers, Pieter was the better, and, according to Waagen, his works often approach those of Philips; "the essential difference between them," adds the German critic, "lies in Pieter's heavier tone of colouring and inferior freedom and spirit of handling." Nicolas Ficke, Jacob Warnars, A. de Haen, and Koort Witholt, a Swede, were also imitators of Philips Wouwerman, and some of their pictures have been probably often passed off by dishonest dealers on the ignorant or unwary art purchaser as original works by Philips Wouwerman.

ISACK JANSZ, VAN OSTADE.

Born 1621.—*Died* 1649.

"WE derive the pleasure of surprise," writes the painter, John Constable, "from the works of the best Dutch painters in finding how much interest Art, when in perfection, can give to the most ordinary subjects." This pleasure of surprise is especially given by the unpretending scenes of rural life that the brothers Van Ostade depicted with such consummate taste.

In one, a frozen canal is shown with boys skating across ; in another, a market woman is vending her wares ; in a third, peasants are drinking and singing under the trellised porch of a rustic cottage : out of such every-day scenes and occupations Adriaan and Isack * van Ostade drew pictures worthy to hang by the side of the creations of the greatest masters. "*Otez moi ces magots*," exclaimed Louis XIV., when some of those Dutch figure-pictures were laid before him ; but how surprised his periwigged Majesty would be could he revisit his Palace of the Louvre, and see places of honour given to these same *magots*, and to find that the most artistic of people had placed these and similar

---

* Or Izaak ; but the above is the more correct form.

paintings in the *salon carré* itself, and that Van Ostade, Teniers, and Dou rubbed frames with Leonardo and Raphael, Titian and Correggio.

Isack van Ostade was not appreciated, nor his merits descried until the close of last century ; probably his more famous brother's reputation made that of Isack pale before it. In Descamps's *Lives of the Flemish Painters* Isack is dismissed with but one line of notice, and the same is the case in Balkema's work, where Isack is merely alluded to as having been a pupil of his brother Adriaan, and that his pictures were inferior to those of the latter, but he adds that some of Isack's works are admired.

John Smith, a much later writer on Dutch art than the authors just mentioned, pays a fairer tribute to the qualities of Isack van Ostade's talent, for he says that the excellence of some of Isack's pictures places him in the same rank with his brother Adriaan, and he adds his belief that had Isack's life been prolonged he might have acquired an equally extended reputation. As in the case of Jan Steen and others of the great Dutch painters, it was the English who first appreciated Isack van Ostade's delightful little pictures, which have the rare merit of combining in almost equal measure both landscape and figure-painting. It is difficult to know which to admire the most, the truth of his winter scenes, wayside landscapes, and luminous skies, or the admirably grouped and perfectly drawn figures that animate them. As a colourist Isack is inferior to his brother Adriaan ; he indulged too much in deep brown shadows and his flesh tones are somewhat yellow, and occasionally his figures are painted in rather a hard style ; but these defects sink into insignificance compared to this painter's sterling merits both as a landscape and a figure-painter.

A VILLAGE SCENE.
BY ISACK VAN OSTADE.

Isack, who was nearly eleven years younger than his brother Adriaan, was born at Haarlem in 1621. Very little has been recorded regarding Isack's industrious life; we only know that he studied under his elder brother, whose style he imitated, and whose same subjects —the interiors of alehouses and taverns, crowded with gambling, drinking, fighting boors — he also painted. He, too, adopted the name of Van Ostade, and so signed himself on his paintings.

Luckily for his fame Isack soon discovered that he could do little good if he only painted similar scenes to those of his brother Adriaan, and he struck out a fresh path for himself. A craving seems to have taken him to leave the heated, tainted air of the beer-houses, and to breathe a better and a purer atmosphere. In his second manner, he takes us out of the tobacco-smoke of the taverns into the green fields and under the bright skies; the air is redolent with brine as we watch him painting the sands and boats at Scheveningen, or glide over the frozen canal alive with skaters; and fresh and clear and full of life we watch the heavily-laden van with its living freight as it stops by the wayside inn : a merry group of peasants dance to the accompaniment of a pipe and a blind fiddler : the old grey horse is being cared for, and is drinking his fill from out the lichen-covered old trough : dogs scamper yelping over the common, while fresh arrivals jog in, some on foot, some on horseback, some in covered carts—eagerly hurrying on to enjoy their much longed-for mid-day rest.

One might write chapters about these delightful pictures, each a little idyl in itself ; they prove that the man who painted them must have been by nature a poet, a true and fervent lover and worshipper of nature. Would that

we knew more about this painter's career ; probably he
lived a quiet, uneventful life in Haarlem, where, too soon,
he died, in 1649.*

Isack van Ostade's pictures are very scarce. As has already
been said, he was first appreciated as he deserved in this
country : hence there are more of his works in the private
collections of England than in the public galleries of
Europe. The Louvre contains four examples : two of these
are travellers halting at wayside inns, the two others are
winter subjects. There are only two of his works in the Amsterdam Gallery ; only single specimens at the Antwerp and
Vienna Galleries ; the Hermitage at St. Petersburg, however,
has five ; and there are two in the Gallery at Brussels.
We have in our National Gallery three fine examples of
Isack's talent ; one, a winter scene, is a splendid specimen.
In Lord Ashburton's Collection is a fine picture of an
evening effect, and there is a painting by this artist in
Lord Northbrook's Collection.   In the Royal Collection are
a pair, there are also two in the Bridgewater Gallery ; and
in Lansdowne House is another—one of his many winter
scenes.

* M. van der Willigen and other authorities give 1657 ; but Dr.
Meyer and Dr. Bode, in their catalogue of the Berlin Gallery (1873),
say 1649.

JAN STEEN.

Born 1626.—*Died* 1679.

F EW painters have suffered so much at the hands of
their biographers as Jan Steen. He has been
represented as more of a drunkard than a painter, as a
keeper of a tavern frequented by low, dissolute persons, in
whose company he is said to have wasted his time rather
than employ it in the execution of his art. But the
number of authentic works by him—about five hundred—
is alone sufficient to refute the charge.

The circumstances of his life are enveloped in hopeless
confusion. By some writers he is said to have been a
brewer only, and not a keeper of an ale-house; by others,
that he had a brewery is denied, while his ownership of an
ale-house is upheld. And, again, the scene of his labours
in various years is the subject of much controversy. But
all modern writers agree in denouncing the great injustice
done to the memory of Jan Steen by early chroniclers in
representing him as a drunken profligate. The true facts
of his life—*so far as they are known*—are due to the pains-
taking researches of M.M. Van der Willigen, Christiaan
Kramm, and Rammelman-Elsevier; but, above all, to those
of M. T. van Westrheene, who has published an excellent
monograph on him.

F P II   E

Jan Havicksz Steen was born at Leyden in 1626, the year following the marriage of his parents. His father, Havick Jansz Steen, who was in all probability a brewer, was of respectable family, and in good circumstances. Jan's mother was Elisabeth Wijbrantsd Capiteijns. Noticing the precocious talents of the young Jan, his father sent him to study under one Nicolas Knuffer (or Knupfer), a German painter of historical subjects, settled at Utrecht. Jan then probably went to Haarlem and entered the studio of Adriaan van Ostade, the influence of whose style is, at any rate, perceptible in many of his works. Adriaan Brouwer has, without sufficient reason, also been mentioned among the names of his instructors in art. Steen's last master was Van Goijen, of the Hague, whose daughter, Margaretha, he married there in 1649 ; he had been inscribed in the Painters' Guild at Leyden in the previous year. Four, if not five, children were the result of this marriage. Steen, it appears, was absent from Leyden from 1649 to 1653, from 1653 to 1658, and from 1658 to 1672, during which period many of his best works were painted. Perhaps some years after 1649 were spent at the Hague. That he resided at Haarlem at various times from 1661 to 1669 is more than probable, for M. Van der Willigen has found the records of the birth and early burial there of an infant daughter in 1662, of the burial of his wife there in 1669, and another record to the effect that poor Steen had some of his pictures seized and sold by an apothecary in payment of a debt of " 10 florins, 5 sous, and 8 deniers," contracted for medicine during his wife's illness. The same writer tells us that Steen agreed to give—in payment of one year's rent (1666-1667) of 29 florins—3 portraits "painted as well as he was able," from which we are led to assume that he was not in the habit of getting very

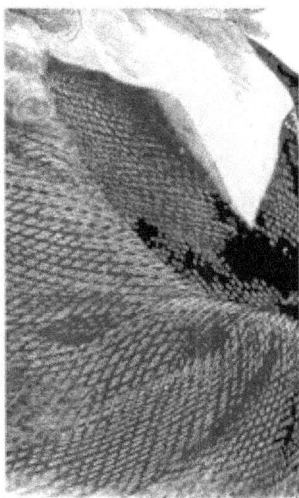

JAN STEEN.

FROM A PAINTING BY HIMSELF.

large sums for his works. M. Van der Willigen also tells us that in 1667 Steen was carrying on the trade of a brewer at Delft. But M. Van Westrheene has searched through all the registers of the Corporation of Brewers of that city for the name of Steen without success. Nor was he more successful in his endeavours to find him mentioned among the painters of Delft.

In 1672 we find Steen back again in Leyden—returned, it is said, to obtain possession of the property left him by his father, who had died in 1669—and in that year, 1672, he applied for and obtained permission from the magistrates to open a tavern, which he established at Langebrug. In 1673 he married for a second time—his choice being Marie van Egmont, widow of one Nicolas Herculens. A son was born in 1674 : five years later, in 1679, Jan Steen died, and was buried in the parish church of St. Peter at Leyden on the 3rd of February, leaving his house, which he had inherited from his father, to his widow and his children.

" What a singular thing it is," writes W. Bürger in his notice of the Museums of Holland, " that it should be the English who have done most to raise the reputation of the dissipated painter." The French critic supports this assertion by giving a list of the different English owners of works by *ce peintre débraillé*—in which occur the names of Lords Ashburton, Ellesmere, Bute, Dudley, Overstone, and half-a-dozen others ; among the number he remarks that *le grand Lord Wellington surtout adorait les Steen*. At the Art Treasures Exhibition in Manchester, Bürger counted no less than eleven Jan Steens, more, he says, than the united galleries of Vienna, Dresden, Munich, and Berlin put together then possessed of this painter's works, and it is more than they possess now.

Were Jan Steen's paintings merely representations of

ale-house scenes it would indeed be strange that he should
have been so popular among the amateurs and collectors
of England, but they are a great deal more than this ; and
although one can not understand what Sir Joshua Reynolds
saw in Steen's paintings to make him write that astounding
statement that Steen's style "might become even the design
of Rafaelle !" no intelligent observer of the Dutch painter's
works can fail to acknowledge that in humour, technical
skill, and originality, Steen has a right to a foremost place
among the greatest painters of his country, and deserves
the high praise bestowed on him by our painter, C. R.
Leslie, who has left on record his opinion that Jan Steen
"was the greatest genius of the Dutch painters of familiar
life."

Take, for instance, that Interior of a School in the Bridgewater Gallery, or the Invalid Lady at Apsley House, or a
Musical Party in the Royal Collection, or above all that
marvellous picture, said to represent the Comedy of Human
Life from its earliest to its latest stages, in the Gallery at
the Hague—pictures such as these have rightly claimed for
Jan Steen the highest fame among the greatest masters of
the Dutch school.

If we compare poetry to painting, Steen is to Rembrandt
what Molière is to Shakespeare. Steen, like Molière, is often
coarse, but always witty. As a draughtsman, Steen is as
correct as Terborch, in colour equal to Metsu, and as
happy in grouping his figures as Van Ostade or De Hooch ;
and although our minds may not be elevated by Steen's
pictures, it is impossible not to laugh with the merry
painter as he brings before our eyes the humours and
drolleries of that serio-comic drama, human life.

In one of his numerous pictures of tavern life he has
represented a scene that reminds one of a similar event in

the Rake's Progress, in which husband and wife appear the morning after a night of cards and dissipation. Steen's picture is less dramatic than Hogarth's, but more real ; we see the jovial painter and his no less jolly wife Margaretha in a tavern, everything in confusion, the furniture upset, the children allowed to romp unchecked, the cat making off with a rasher of bacon, while Steen looks calmly on, tankard in hand, with an expression on his face as if he wished to show his friends the blessings of family life. In scenes such as these, he did not spare himself more than his associates. All his paintings are full of satire, and he lashed his own and his countrymen and women's pleasant vices all alike with that terribly severe brush of his.

Steen resembled Molière in often introducing on his stage, scenes in which the doctor is the hero. How well he has drawn them, those pompous, empty-headed old quacks, with their sombre garb, peaked hats and long gold-topped canes ; and however coarse such scenes and others that he delighted to paint are, there runs, as Leslie remarks, through all Steen's works a something that proves that there must have been good in this eccentric painter. How true to nature are his children ; no one has painted the scenes of childhood with a tenderer or kinder brush. Look at his Feast of St. Nicholas, in the Rotterdam Museum ; it is a subject he was very fond of depicting, for here he could find a large field for the ex-pressions of delight and disappointment in the little faces he painted so well. He who could paint such pictures had doubtless a kind, loving heart, and much good-nature.

Steen deserves a place by the side of Hogarth, whom he strongly resembles in many ways. Both painted the follies and vices of their day ; both lashed these follies and

vices as no other artists of their respective countries did
before, or have been able to do since; both illustrated the
comedy of human life, showing strongly its dark shadows.
Hogarth's object was more pointed; and although Steen
never attempted such a series of works as the Harlot's or
the Rake's Progress, there is almost as much satire in many
of his scenes as in those of the great English humourist.
They are also alike in never showing any morbid dislike to
poor human nature in their paintings, although Steen, like
Hogarth, must have felt how mean, and how trivial, and
how sordid much of humanity is. Like Hogarth also,
Steen failed miserably when he attempted higher flights in
the regions of art, and tried to illustrate sacred or profane
history; the least bad of these attempts is a picture in
the Arenberg Gallery at Brussels, in which Steen has
represented the Miracle of the Water turned into Wine;
it is probable that the subject appealed strongly to the
imagination of the painter. In trying to paint such scenes
as Esther and Ahasuerus, or the Continence of Scipio, or
Anthony and Cleopatra, Steen was as much out of his
element as was Hogarth when he painted Paul before
Felix, or Moses and Pharaoh's Daughter.

Steen has painted himself in various characters. Once
we see him leaning back in a chair playing the guitar, and
singing as though there were no such things as troubles
or cares in the world, and he looks for all time in that
picture what he was, the most jovial, careless Bohemian
that ever quaffed a bowl or wielded painter's brush.

Although Jan Steen died comparatively young, in 1679,
aged fifty-three, he left a large number of works behind. The museums of Holland, as well as some of the
private galleries of England, contain a great number
of his paintings. As we have already said, Steen was a

THE DANCING DOG. BY JAN STEEN.

most unequal artist; some of his paintings are worth great
sums, while others, owing both to their subjects and the
carelessness with which they were painted, are hardly
worthy of finding a better home than the walls of a tavern.

In the Louvre there is only a single painting by Steen.
It represents a feast of peasants; Charles Blanc valued it
at 30,000 francs. In the Gallery of the Belvedere, at
Vienna, are two Steens, and the same number are in
the Munich Gallery. Dresden has three. The Amsterdam Gallery has eleven; among them, the painter's own
portrait. There are seven Steens in the Hague Museum.
In the Gallery of the Hermitage at St. Petersburg there
is a good specimen, one of the many pictures in which
Steen has introduced a doctor and a fair patient. The
Galleries of Berlin, of Frankfort, of Antwerp, Brussels,
and Florence have each and all examples of this master,
and even in the provincial French museums, such as Rouen,
Nantes, and Montpellier, Steen's pictures are to be met
with. There are also many in the private French galleries.
In our English private galleries Jan Steen takes a high
place, notably at Apsley House and in the Bridgewater
Gallery. There is a fine Steen in the National Gallery
which was formerly in the Peel Collection.

Many of Jan Steen's drawings exist, scattered among
private collections; they are full of cleverness and spirit,
and prove that he was as ready with his pencil as with
his brush.

M. van Westrheene gives a list of 482 works by Steen,
of which 201 are in the public and private collections of
Europe. The whereabouts of the rest he has been unable
to discover.

GABRIEL METSU.

Born 1630—*Living as late as* 1667.

BÜRGER remarks, in his *Dutch Galleries*, that those who have studied the paintings of Metsu, Terborch, or Caspar Netscher will be able to form a better idea of the manners and customs of the Dutch in the seventeenth century than could be obtained by poring over a whole library of books of archæology, history or biography. The Van Ostadès, Jan Steens, and the Brouwers show us what may be called the vulgar side of this Dutch seventeenth century life, while Terborch, Netscher, Mieris, and Metsu take us into the dwellings of the rich and the refined. With the latter we see the inner life of the fair dames and their admirers, all in rich and rare costumes, rustling in satins and brocades. We admire the hangings and furniture of their dwellings, the walls all aglow with stamped leather relieved by the black ebony frames of the mirrors, the great carved marble chimney, the brocaded bed-hangings, and richly-decorated cabinets and wardrobes. How polished are those cavaliers, in their long locks, steenkirk cravats, and golden baldrics; how clean and neat the close fitting cap of the maid; how trim the page, with the silver salver on which the cut lemon is waiting to be squeezed into the embossed tankard. Or still, accompanied by these refined folk, we take an airing under the limes of the "Maliebaan," or Mall; or visit the busy market-place, and stroll along the sides of the canal alive with boats and barges; the heavy gables of the red-brick houses on the other side throwing their bright reflections in the still waters below. Thus, these magicians of the palette and the brush take us back two centuries and more, and show us the way these people lived in that little land reclaimed from the sea, which behind its artificial dykes bred and nourished so warlike and so valiant a race—a race of men that defied all the might and power and wealth of Spain and the Indies; that held its own against the arms of the Grand Monarque; a race whose fleets swept the seas of two hemispheres; of men who for one short century seemed to combine the qualities that had made Greece the mother of the arts, and Rome the mistress of the world.

Leyden, that town that may well be called the cradle of Dutch art, claims, amongst her illustrious sons, Gabriel Metsu.* Of his life we know but little. Born at Leyden in 1630, he was the son of Jacques Metsu, a native of Belle, in Flanders, and of his third wife Jacomina Garnijerns, widow of a painter Willem Fremault. Gabriel's first instructor in art was probably his father, who was a painter of no great note: he then studied under Gerard Dou; and from his works we gather that the style of Terborch must have, more or less, had an effect upon Metsu's manner. He was admitted into the Guild of Painters at Leyden in 1648, but he left that city two years later and went to Amsterdam; there he settled, and there he probably spent the greater part of his life. From an inscription † on a picture, of the year 1662 (No. 1307 in

---

* Sometimes written Metzu.

† Vrilje (vrijwillige), Verkoping-Hofstede-Maersen.

he Dresden Gallery), it has been suggested that he some-
imes passed the summer months at Maarsen, a village
etween Utrecht and Amsterdam. In 1658 * he married
sabella Wolff, and in the following year he obtained the
ight of citizenship of Amsterdam. The dates on his
pictures prove that he was still living in 1667. Research
ias failed to find any record of his death.

Smith, in his *Catalogue Raisonné* of Dutch artists,
ias compared Metsu to Van Dyck; but as Metsu
carcely ever painted any scene but those taken from
.omestic life, and always on a small scale, the comparison
eems to us rather far-fetched. Metsu's figures certainly
re full of grace and refinement, and his colouring is free
nd brilliant. In some respects, Metsu's paintings are
qual to Gerard Dou's; they often surpass those of Mieris
oth in gracefulness and in expression. No one (Terborch
xcepted), could better paint a silk or a satin dress.
Metsu's works have always commanded a great and wide
opularity, and this is easily understood, as his subjects
re always refined and pleasant to look upon and to live
vith. His pictures are found in all the principal European
ublic galleries, and many are present in our collections.
There exist between 120 and 130 of his paintings. In the
Louvre there are eight; the best of these is a view of the
Vegetable Market at Amsterdam, which was sold, more
han a century ago, for 28,000 livres. One of the others
t the Louvre represents the Woman taken in Adultery,
nd is interesting from being one of the very few Biblical
ubjects that Metsu attempted, and which, it is scarcely
iecessary to add, is a decided failure. The Dresden Gal-
ery contains seven Metsus, all of good quality. In the

* The year formerly given for his death.

Belvedere at Vienna there is a fine specimen ; he has also several works in the galleries of the Hague and at Amsterdam ; there is also a fine Metsu in the gallery at Cassel. In the Hermitage Gallery are three superb specimens, and in the Suermondt Collection in the Berlin Museum there is a remarkably fine life-size portrait of a lady by Metsu, which is said to represent his mother.

The National Gallery has three of his works. Among the finest specimens in our private galleries we would especially mention four in the Queen's Collection at Buckingham Palace ; one of these represents a man playing on a violoncello, and in another the painter has drawn his own portrait. Lord Northbrook's fine Metsu, and two of his works at Bridgewater House, show his different styles : the Stirrup Cup, dark in tone, and the Fishwife, wonderfully brilliant in colour ; the fish it seems almost possible to smell and touch. There is also a Metsu in Lord Bute's Collection.

Formerly, many Metsus existed in French private collections, but most of these have left France in recent years. There was a famous picture by this artist in Cardinal Fesch's Gallery, which was sold at Rome, in 1845, for more than 74,000 francs. M. Delepert has also a fine work by this master.

At Copenhagen, the Count A. G. de Moltke has a superb picture by him. It is uncertain whether Metsu had pupils ; but for a fact the mysterious Ver Meer, of Delft, imitated Metsu's manner closely, painting also similar subjects, but in a bolder and larger manner.

Uchterveldt and Michiel van Musscher were both pupils of Gabriel Metsu.

NICOLAAS MAES.

Born 1632.—*Died* 1693.

WE should feel puzzled if we had the choice given us between a good example of Pieter de Hooch and one of Nicolaas Maes's pictures. There is much likeness in the subjects which these two charming painters placed on their canvases; much resemblance between them also in the superb colouring and perfect grouping of their figures: these two artists, with Ver Meer, of Delft, have in their way never been surpassed, and it would be no easy question to answer which is the greatest of the three.

It is a matter of doubt whether De Hooch and Ver Meer were pupils of Rembrandt, but it is certain that Maes studied under him. During his lifetime, and until the end of last century, Maes was chiefly known as a portrait painter. When he visited Jordaens at Antwerp, he was questioned by that artist what manner of painting he practised. Maes replied, "I am but a portrait painter." His reputation is, however, not now maintained by his portraits, which are inferior to Honthorst's, but rests on the superb little pictures of scenes from every-day life—a Dutch housewife nursing her child; or surprising her maid asleep over her pots and pans; a girl leaning out of window, or

listening to a group of lovers who imagine they are un-
watched and unheard ; an old woman saying grace, or peeling potatoes ; a child knitting a stocking ; an old man
reading a book ; and other similar subjects. To these
simple scenes Maes gave a charm and a beauty that only
two or three painters have ever equalled ; as Charles
Blanc observes, his colouring is as fine as that of Rembrandt and of Titian.

Nicolaas Maes* was born at Dordrecht (or Dort) in 1632.
Aalbert Cuyp, Ferdinand Bol, and Godfried Schalken were
all born in or near this most artistic town. There is,
we believe, but one of his works in his native city, but his
fame has slowly spread wherever true art is appreciated.
We know little about his life. M. Bürger imagines that
his best works were produced while he worked in Rembrandt's studio, between his twentieth and twenty-fifth
year; it is certain that the withdrawal of the influence
of the master had a most unfortunate effect on his later
works. Until 1660 all that he painted bore a firmness of
touch, a rich impasto, a splendour of colour, that in later
years he seems to have lost or forgotten. So remarkable
is this change, and so great is the falling-off in his later
works, principally portraits, as compared with his early
genre pictures, that it has been supposed that portraits of
more recent date are not by the same artist, but are the
performances of some other Maes, a name not at all un-
common in Holland, and which not unfrequently occurs
among the artistic records of that country, as in the case
of, for instance, Dirk Maas, a pupil of Mommers, and
another, one Godefroid Maes of Antwerp.

After quitting Rembrandt's studio Maes left Amsterdam and went to Antwerp, probably about 1660-1665.

* Or Maas.

THE IDLE SERVANT.
By Nicolaas Maes.

The great painters of the Flemish School — those giants of colour and composition, were all dead—Rubens in 1640, Van Dyck in the following year, Snyders in 1657; and when Maes went to Antwerp the Flemish School was rapidly declining. Jordaens and Teniers were almost the only survivors of the great days of the art of Flanders.

According to Descamps, Maes was a most successful portrait painter; he had found out the secret of success in that branch of art—an infallible one—that of flattery. Like Netscher, Maes was a martyr to the gout; he died of this complaint in his sixty-first year, in 1693, at Amsterdam, to which city he had returned and settled in 1678.

Extremely rare are Maes's pictures; only about fifty are known to exist in the public and private galleries of Europe. Our National Gallery is fortunate in possessing three very fine specimens—The Cradle, The Dutch Housewife, and The Idle Servant. Two of Maes's portraits are in the Munich Gallery, two in the Museum at Amsterdam, and other examples exist in the Six and Van der Hoop collections. In the Gallery of the Hermitage, St. Petersburg, are two; and there is a fine life-size portrait, named The Philosopher, in the Berlin Gallery. There are some fine examples of Maes's talent in our private collections; in the royal collection at Buckingham Palace is a very good one; in the Bridgewater Gallery also there is a charming work by Maes—representing a girl knitting —of intense depth and brilliant tone of colour. Sir Richard Wallace has a fine Maes in his splendid collection; at Lansdowne House is likewise a good specimen of this gifted artist's talent.

The painter C. R. Leslie says on the subject of Maes's

paintings, "There are few pictures in our National Gallery before which I find myself more often standing than the very small one by him, the subject of which is the scraping a parsnip. A decent-looking Dutch housewife sits intently engaged in this operation, with a fine chubby child standing by her side watching the process, as children will stand and watch the most ordinary operations, with an intensity of interest as if the very existence of the whole world depended upon the exact manner in which that parsnip was scraped. It is not the light and colour of this charming little gem, superlative as they are, that constitute its great attraction; for a mere outline of it would arrest attention among a thousand subjects of its class, and many pictures as beautiful in effect might not interest so much; but it is the delight at seeing a trait of childhood we have often observed and been amused with in Nature, for the first time so felicitously given by Art."

JAN VER MEER, OF DELFT.

Born 1632.—*Died* 1696.

THE little we know respecting the mysterious painter whose name stands above—an artist of extraordinary talent—we owe to the researches of a French critic, who under the *nom de plume* of Bürger * wrote a most interesting work on the Museums of Holland.

Up to the time that Bürger's book was published, but few even of those who had studied Dutch art appeared to know that in Ver Meer of Delft the Dutch school possessed a master almost equal in effect to De Hooch, and equal, if not superior, to Nicolaas Maes and Gabriel Metsu. Descamps, in his *Lives of the Dutch Artists,* makes no allusion to Ver Meer; this seems strange, for it is certain that his paintings were sold for considerable sums in his lifetime.

The artist's name is, in itself, a difficulty and a cause of confusion, for at the same time as he lived, flourished two other painters bearing the same, or very nearly similar, names. These were Ver Meer, or Van der Meer, of Haarlem, and Ver Meer of Utrecht; the former called of Haarlem, that being the place of his birth, the latter

---

* His real name was Thoré.

of Utrecht, that town being the place of his adoption ; he was born at Schoonhoven.

Our painter was known to his fellow-countrymen as the " Delftsche Van der Meer," having been born in the town of Delft in 1632. Tradition asserts that Ver Meer * studied with Karel Fabritius ; and after that painter's death in 1654, he visited Amsterdam and worked under the eye of Rembrandt. He was certainly at his native city of Delft in the years 1662, 1663, 1670 ; and in 1671, as his name appears among the members of the Painters' Guild for that year, by the side of those of Palamedesz and others ; he had been elected as a master painter in 1653 : but these are all the meagre scraps of information that we can find. concerning one of the most remarkable painters of the Dutch school. His death probably took place at Delft in 1696, for in that year a sale took place of twenty-one of his works.

No one who has visited the Hague Museum can fail to have admired a large landscape of astonishing force, evidently the work of a master hand. This long landscape is a view of the artist's birthplace—picturesque old Delft, with its red brick buildings reflected in the still waters of its canals : it is a landscape, or rather a townscape, that puts one in mind of some of Millais's wonderfully vivid transcripts of nature ; we feel we are looking, not at a picture, but at a real view. It is by Ver Meer.

Another landscape, of a very different scene, by Ver Meer, is a recently acquired treasure in the Suermondt Collection, in the Berlin Gallery. This painting represents a wild tract of open country, and is remarkable for the

* Commonly, but incorrectly, written Van der Meer. He is inscribed in the register of the Guild of St. Luke as Vermeer ; and so —or sometimes J. V. Meer—he signed his name.

A DUTCH FAMILY.

By Jan van der Meer of Delft.
In the Gallery of the Academy at Vienna.

fine feeling and broad treatment displayed by the artist. Here, in this again, one is put in mind of Millais; Ver Meer of Delft seems to have been capable of painting everything he saw; with the same success he could represent either the long sweep of a distant horizon, the bricks of a house, the lace of a gown, or the lights and shades on a woman's face, and the expression of her mouth and eyes : he could represent all these different objects with equal truth to nature, and equal skill in their portrayal.

In the Arenberg Gallery at Brussels is a girl's head, worthy of Rembrandt; it is the work of Ver Meer of Delft.

In the Queen's Collection at Windsor Castle is a little *genre* painting, a lady playing on a harpsichord, as exquisite in colour, tone, and finish as a Gerard Dou, a Metsu, or a Mieris; this is the work of Jan Ver Meer. At the Gallery of the Hermitage at St. Petersburg is a picture of still life—dead game, fruit, etc., painted in a manner worthy of Snyders; this also is a work of Ver Meer. Only about a dozen of this painter's works are known, and these are scattered in the different galleries of Europe; besides the large view of Delft at the Hague Museum to which we have alluded, there are two fine specimens by Ver Meer in the Six Collection at Amsterdam, another in the Van der Hoop Gallery. In the Gallery at Dresden are a couple; one of these is a life-size group of half a dozen half-length figures; it is the only life-size painting that exists by Ver Meer, and we must confess to having felt some disappointment when we saw it; it is coarse as compared to his former works. The subject of this painting is what, for want of a better term, is called a "conversation piece," a scene such as Valentin delighted in portraying, and is certainly equal in vivacity and spirit

to the works of that artist. The other—a smaller work—
shows a young woman reading a letter at an open window,
somewhat too blue in the flesh tones; this strange love
for blue in the flesh tints is also shown in a little cabinet
picture by Ver Meer in the Gallery of the Louvre,
of a Woman making Lace; and this is also the case
with a picture by him in the Berlin Gallery, a Girl
dressing before a Mirror. Perhaps this blueness is the
result of injudicious cleaning and restoring; but this
painter had a great partiality for bringing in two colours
in all his pictures, a deep blue and a lemon yellow, and
nearly all his female figures are clad in one or both of
these, his favourite colours.

A very few of Ver Meer's pictures are in the private
collections of England and the Continent. Within the
last year or two Lord Powerscourt was fortunate enough
to secure a beautiful little picture by Ver Meer at a sale at
Christie's. We believe it highly probable that there are
still many pictures by Ver Meer still to be discovered,
hidden away in some neglected gallery, or some old
country-house; and perhaps if search were made, a picture
that has passed for generations as the work of Metsu or
Maes, might prove to be by the mysterious old painter
of Delft. Unfortunately M. Bürger no longer exists to
search for, and gather fresh, information regarding
his favourite Ver Meer — "a sphinx" as he not
inappropriately calls him.

PIETER DE HOOCH.

Born 1632 (?).—*Died* 1681 (?).

THAT eminent painter, C. R. Leslie, says that De Hooch is, with the exception of Rembrandt, the most original painter of the Dutch School. One might add that not only is De Hooch one of the most original of Dutch painters, but one of the most original artists of any time, school, or country.

Pieter de Hooch* was born at Rotterdam, apparently on the 12th of June, 1632. His style was formed from a study of the works of Karel Fabritius and of Rembrandt. He worked at Delft and at Haarlem, where he died it is said in 1681.† What his outward man was like we can tell by the portrait he has left of himself, in the Amsterdam Gallery; in which we see a young man with a pale, thoughtful countenance of the Calvinistic type, with long straight hair lying low on a wide turned-down collar. This youth with the deep sad eyes is De Hooch in his twentieth year.

Two other Dutch painters of signal merit—Aalbert

---

* Or Hooche, Hooghe, Hoogh, or Hooge.

† "His biography can only be gathered from the occasional dates of his pictures extending from 1656 to 1670."—KUGLER's *Handbook*, edited by J. A. Crowe.

Cuyp and Meindert Hobbema shared the fate of De
Hooch in not being appreciated in their lifetimes, nor
indeed for nearly a century after their deaths. It seems
passing strange now that the picture dealers of a century
ago should have erased the signatures from the immortal
paintings and substituted the names of other artists, in
order that what De Hooch and Hobbema had painted
should not take up needless space in their sale rooms.

In his able work on the Dutch Galleries, Bürger calls
attention to the likeness evident in Adriaan van Ostade's
paintings and those of De Hooch to Rembrandt's style, and
infers from this resemblance that both studied under that
great master. Whether or not De Hooch was a pupil of
Rembrandt's can add little to our admiration for the rare
talent that his few, and now almost priceless, pictures dis-
play. Claude himself does not convey with greater power
the idea of sunlight than do many of De Hooch's works. In
our National Gallery are a couple of this artist's finest
paintings ; the subjects are simple enough, merely the
interiors of two Dutch houses, but painted with such
wondrous truth that when one looks at them one is con-
vinced that never was sunlight more marvellously rendered,
and one feels almost willing to forget that only a painted
surface is before one's eyes, and not a veritable scene in
a quiet old Dutch house. Out of Holland, De Hooch's
paintings are extremely scarce ; and even in that country
they are among the rarest art treasures in the public and
private galleries.

At the Louvre there are but two examples ; one of these
represents a richly decorated room, in which by the side of
a superbly sculptured fire-place a group are engaged over
their cards ; it is a splended picture, a delight and a wonder
—how full this rich chamber is of light, yet how much more

seems to be kept out by that heavy curtain beyond the card-
players, near which a couple are eagerly conversing! How
delicately every detail is painted, down to the lady's little
foot so gracefully placed on the black and white marble of
the floor, how skilfully the light is reflected on the golden
stamped leather of the walls, how noiselessly the page
enters from the outer room, with his salver and glass and
flask of wine. This is a picture of "high life:" De Hooch's
representations of "low life" are equally beautiful, but it
can hardly be said that De Hooch, like Brouwer or Steen,
ever painted really low life, all that his magic brush
touched, however humble, he ennobled. Look at that
modest little red-brick paved courtyard of a Dutch house
in our National Gallery—the people who live here are poor;
here are no pages, on the walls no stamped leather, but this
matron with her household duties and the clean red tiles
and whitewashed walls are, owing to this artist's genius,
as beautiful and as delightful to look on as that richly
furnished room and the aristocratic company in the high
life picture at the Louvre. What a feeling of peace and
comfort the humbler home conveys! how neat and trim the
housewife looks as she sits in the cool shadow of the yard,
half busied with some domestic task, half watching her
little girl at play on the red tiled floor; while out in the
sun-lit court an old man passes, throwing a heavy shadow
across the whitewashed wall. In these pictures by De Hooch,
it seems always afternoon. Remark how this painter
conquered what to many other artists has been an insur-
mountable difficulty, namely, the rendering of the different
gradations of light—first a cool darkened room is shown,
then beyond this a passage in which the light is bright
and warm, but how different to the glare beyond, outside
in the quiet and sunny old street, the trees along the slow

canal look cool and shady ; but how hot the tall red gables, all aglow with the strong light of the setting sun, sinking in the western sky. Sometimes, but very rarely, De Hooch takes us out of doors, as in a picture showing us a couple seated in the sunshine ; but whether within or out of doors we feel at home and at peace with this pleasant, good-natured painter, whose pictures are so well known to us, but of whose personal life we know so little.

In looking at this artist's works one feels certain that he who painted these sunny, happy, innocent pictures must have been a refined and gentle man, a man fond of children and flowers, of music and of sunshine, one who could see and also convey to others by his rare talent, the happy truth that to a pure mind and a good heart nothing under God's Heaven need be unsightly or useless, and that in all things that He made, something of beauty is to be found, to those who look for it with reverent and thankful eyes.

The indefatigable Smith in his *Catalogue Raisonné* of the Dutch painters, notes sixty-eight of De Hooch's paintings, most of those are in private collections. Besides those already mentioned at the Louvre, and in the National Gallery, the Museum at Amsterdam has two, one the painter's portrait, the other known by the title of the Buttery Hatch. The Van der Hoop Gallery rejoices in five De Hoochs : there are also examples in the Six Collection.

At Buckingham Palace there are two superb De Hoochs, but not superior to the three in the National Gallery, which are in themselves enough to have made this painter im-mortal. Sir Richard Wallace has a fine De Hooch, and there are others which are reckoned with reason among the gems of our private galleries. We English were the first to appreciate this great artist, whose tardy recognition in his own country bears out the scriptural adage.

FRANS VAN MIERIS.

Born 1635.—*Died* 1681.

GERARD DOU'S best pupil, a jovial, stout, and honest-looking Dutch burgher, was almost his rival, when, in the year 1665, at the age of thirty, he painted his wife's and his own portrait, still to be seen in undimmed colours in the Museum at the Hague.

Mieris was born in 1635, in the quaint old town of Delft, which has given not a few first-rate artists to Holland. He was one of twenty-three children. His father was Jan Bastiaensz van Mieris, a lapidary, and his mother Curina van der Kok. Like his master Dou, he was in early youth apprenticed to a glass-painter, one Abraham Torenvliet. He soon left the glass-painter's studio for that of Gerard Dou, when he gained the title from that painter of the Prince of his Pupils; and this name he fully merited, for some of Mieris's works are as finished in manner as those of Dou. Later on, he studied historical painting under Abraham Tempel; but Dou's influence was triumphant, and when, thanks to the patronage of the Archduke Leopold William, Mieris began to work independently of any teacher, he proved the power of his brush by painting a work that ranks among the *chefs d'œuvre* of the Dutch school, *La Marchande de Soieries*, a comely young damsel showing silks and satins to a some-what forward gallant. The light and shade in this paint-ing are equal to a Dou. Pictures of similar subjects quickly followed. Mieris soon became the most popular painter of *genre* pictures in Holland. Amateurs competed eagerly for these highly-finished little cabinet pictures. No less a potentate than the Grand Duke of Tuscany, finding that no owner of a Mieris would part with one, even at the most extravagant price, went himself to the painter's studio, and chose an unfinished study.

We know little of his personal history and can only add that Mieris died at Leyden on the 12th of March, 1681.

Mieris was essentially a prince's painter; he loved to represent silks and satins, velvets and brocades, massive plate and rich jewels. He shows us the refine-ments of wealth in which the Dutch of the seventeenth century revelled. No other people understood better than they how to make their homes beautiful. We wonder if the gallants of Whitehall or Versailles lived more luxuri-ously than these cavaliers of the Hague and Amsterdam, or if the beauties of Hampton Court and Marly wore larger pearls or more costly silks than the fair ringleted dames whose forms Mieris's brush has preserved for all time! In seeking beautiful forms and splendid objects, Mieris was unlike the generality of the other figure painters of his day in Holland, for whereas Dou and Steen preferred to paint an old market-woman or a dirty child, the courtly Mieris scarcely ever left the polished floor of a saloon hung with stamped leather, and bright with marbles, gilding, and paintings.

FRANS VAN MIERIS IN HIS STUDIO.

From a Painting by Himself.

In the Dresden Gallery.

Looking at these brilliant little pictures of refined life, at these velvet-clad cavaliers, and at these ladies in their satins and swansdown, at the lovely children blowing soap-bubbles across a damask curtain, at these rooms filled with great wine coolers and silver flagons, one would imagine that the painter, who loved to represent these scenes of soft living and voluptuous ease, would have himself been like one of the fine gentlemen he so often painted. Tradition, which is probably most unjust, tells us that Mieris was not at all that sort of man; but we can not believe that one who did not attain the age of fifty, and who has left so many and such finished works, could have been, as some of his contemporaries state, a debauchee; yet, from his being a friend and companion of that marvellously clever, but terribly abused, Jan Steen, Mieris contracted an evil reputation, which has not been removed by a fable of his having tumbled one night into a canal from which he was with difficulty rescued—an immersion that, it is said, led to his death! Mieris was a successful portrait painter, and, like his master Dou, was fond of painting his own portrait. He appears in different costumes; in one as a cavalier, as a trumpeter in another, and in his studio with his wife and maid in a third.

Some confusion has arisen respecting Mieris's pictures, for his sons, Jan and Willem, copied his style, and his grandson (Willem's son) was also named Frans, and closely imitated his grandfather's style; but after carefully studying such a work of the elder Mieris as the exquisite little portrait of a young woman at her toilet in the Bridgewater Collection, or the same lady, probably the painter's wife, feeding a parrot, in the National Gallery, we can not fail to see the superiority of the elder Mieris's skill compared to that of his sons and grandson.

Florence is rich in this painter's works, nine of the elder Mieris's paintings being in the Uffizi Gallery. In the Museum at the Hague are three of his works, a Boy blowing Soap-bubbles, a portrait of Dr. Schuijl, and portraits of the painter and his wife together. Dresden has one of the largest collections of his paintings; in that Gallery there are no less than fifteen. The Louvre contains a fine portrait; and at Munich are some exquisite specimens of his work, including a portrait of himself. And at Buckingham Palace are four of his paintings, one of which is a portrait of the artist and his wife. One solitary etching is ascribed to Frans van Mieris: it represents a sleeping dog.

Besides his sons Willem and Jan, Frans van Mieris had distinguished disciples in Karel de Moor and Arie de Vos.

CASPAR NETSCHER.

Born 1639.—*Died* 1684.

W E think it would be easy for the eye to tire of this
painter's works, and to feel that, like some tooth-
some dishes, a picture by Netscher may go a long way;
perhaps it is as well for the artistic gastronome that there
are but few Netschers in the collections of England and
the Continent.

Caspar Netscher was essentially the painter of what in
old-fashioned English art-books are described as "conversation pieces," in which richly costumed men and
women, in all the heavy gorgeousness of the fashions
of the time of William and Mary and the court of
Versailles, are engaged in the social banalities and cour-
tesies of their artificial lives. In one picture Netscher
has given us the elaborately curled gallant superintending ·
a young lady's lesson in the double-bass; a page attends,
with hat in hand. Again, in another painting, we see a
pair of lovely children seated at an open window, laughing
as they shake their soft curls out of their eyes, and intently watching the soap-bubbles as they mount all green
and purple and lilac in the air; on the carved stone

window-sill, on which the children place their little dim-
pled hands, there is a sculptured frieze of frolicsome goats
and tricksy cupids frightening each other with huge
bearded masks.   And in a third, the painter has grouped
himself and his buxom wife, in a long stomacher, her
ample neck girt with a necklace of pearls, and between
them, with apple in hand, sits their child.   The artist is
a somewhat sad, sickly-looking man, of some forty years :
Netscher was all his life an invalid, and died of the
illness that killed Samuel Pepys, and which had then
no Sir Henry Thompson to crush it.

What an art this of painting is, which allows the
painter and his family to look out at us from this little
picture, only a few inches square, as if they lived again,
although they have been dust and ashes for nearly two
hundred years !

Netscher was born at Heidelberg in 1639 ; he appeared
at a time and in a place all distraught with that most
terrible of calamities, a religious war.   According to
the place of his birth, he was properly not a Dutchman,
but a German ; but, like Lingelbach and Abraham
Mignon, he was only German by birth, and, like them,
lived the greater part of his life and made his fame in Holland, and ranks with these others as one of the great Dutch
painters.   Netscher's father, who had been a sculptor at
Stuttgardt, died young ; his mother was Elizabeth Vetter,
the daughter of a burgomaster of Heidelberg.   Forced to
fly before the Swedish army, the poor woman, who was a
Roman Catholic, fled for shelter with three young children
to a fortress which, surrounded by the enemy, yielded at
length to famine.   When the siege was over, the poor
creature had but one of her children left; this was Caspar:
the others had perished from starvation in her sight.

THE MUSIC LESSON.
By Caspar Netscher.

We next hear of the poor refugees at Arnheim, where a
umane doctor of the name of Tullekens took pity on the
nfortunate mother and little Caspar, whose education he
ndertook to provide. Although the good man hoped that
oung Netscher would follow his profession of medicine,
ae boy evinced so strong a turn for drawing, that Tulle-
ens sent him to study art with a local painter, of still-life,
amed Koster; and from Koster's studio Caspar eventually
etook himself to the famous portrait painter Terborch, at
)eventer. The influence exercised by that great artist
n Netscher is evident in all his best works; although
e lacked the breadth and life-likeness of Terborch,
Setscher has much of his master's pure colouring and
afined feeling; often, however, in his case degenerating
ato weakness from over-finish and over-glazing. When
nly twenty, Netscher was sufficiently skilful with his
rush to set up for himself.

According to Horace Walpole, Netscher, on the invita-
ion of Sir William Temple, paid England a visit; but
[oubraken is silent as regards this event in the artist's
areer, and it is almost certain that he never came to this
ountry; however, we know that Netscher intended to
isit Italy, for on his way thither, when at Bordeaux, in
6.59, he wooed and won Marie, the daughter of a mathe-
latician of that town, Godin of Liége; and, renouncing
is intention of seeing Rome, he returned to the Hague,
hen family cares kept him from thinking of further
ravel. One son, Theodorus, who afterwards became a
ainter, had been born in 1661, before they left Bordeaux.
'aspar was elected a member of the Society of Painters
t the Hague in 1663.

As a portrait painter Netscher had great fame.
Villiam III. especially esteemed him, as we know by

the answer that prince made to the magistrates of Deventer when they asked him to sit for his portrait to Terborch : "I have sat to Netscher; and no one can beat him at a portrait."

Netscher, who, as we have already said, suffered from bad health, died in 1684, at the early age of forty-one, leaving a large fortune to his wife ; and what was of still more importance, sons who worthily upheld the art and fame of the father. The younger—Constantijn—so closely imitated the style of his father, that his paintings have often been mistaken for those of the elder Netscher; but to the connoisseur they lack the marvellous refinement of Caspar's.

It is related of Netscher that not even the gout hindered him from painting, and that he would receive his sitters and paint their portraits even when kept to his bed by pain.

Netscher's paintings are very rare. The Gallery of Dresden has the largest collection of this painter's works, but they only amount to eight. The Louvre contains but two ; in our National Gallery are three fine examples. At the Hermitage, St. Petersburg, are six portraits by him ; and there is in the Bridgewater Gallery a superb little picture by him, supposed to represent the Duchess of Mazarin with St. Evremond.

Besides his two sons, Eglon van der Neer studied under, or at any rate was a close imitator of, Netscher, both as regards the subjects he painted and also the manner. Owing to their great scarceness, Caspar Netscher's pictures, when they come into the market, command prices nearly as high as paintings by Terborch, Mieris, Metsu, or Gerard Dou.

IE PRINCIPAL WORKS OF THE FIGURE PAINTERS OF HOLLAND.

IE following short lists of the works of the Figure Painters of
and have been compiled, for the most part, from the official
ogues of the public galleries of Europe; and the compilers of
catalogues must be held responsible for the authenticity of the
s. The pictures are placed in the lists in the order in which
are mentioned in the catalogues.

GERARD HONTHORST.

:RDAM.	Portrait of William II. G. HONDHORST.
Museum.	Portrait of William II. G. HONTHORST. F. 16—
	Portrait of Prince Frederick Henry of Orange. G. HONTHORST, 1650.
	Portrait of Princess Amalia van Solms-Braunfels, wife of Prince Frederick Henry. G. HONTHORST, 1650. (*The G and the H blended as above, as was his usual custom.*)
	The Happy Musician.
Town Hall.	Portrait of Marie de Medicis. (*Painted in* 1638.)
N. *Museum.*	The Liberation of St. Peter.

BERLIN. *Museum.*	Esau Selling his Birthright.
	The Backgammon-players. G. HONTHORST, F$_t$. 1624.
CASSEL. *Gallery.*	An Old Woman Weighing Gold.
	St. Cecilia.
	A Satyr and Nymph.
	A Musical Party.
COMBE ABBEY.	Portrait of the Queen of Bohemia.
	Portrait of the King of Bohemia.
	Portrait of Charles I.
	Portrait of Prince Rupert.
	Portrait of Gerard Honthorst. (*A bust.*)
COPENHAGEN.	A Family Concert.
Museum.	Diana and her Nymphs. G. HONTHORST FECIT, 1650.
	Female Portrait. . . . HORST.
DRESDEN. *Gall:*	The Dentist.
	Portrait of an Old Woman, with a piece of gold in her han
	Portrait of an Old Woman. (*Bought as a Rembrandt.*)
FLORENCE. *Uffizi.*	Several Persons at Supper
	A Gipsy Telling Fortunes.
	A Supper.
	The Virgin and Child and St. Joseph.
	Adoration of the Shepherds.
	His own Portrait.
HAMPTON COURT.	Duke of Buckingham and Family.
	Christian, Duke of Brunswick.
HAGUE. *Gallery.*	Portrait of William II. of Nassau, Prince of Orange.
	Portraits of Two Young Princesses. (*Probably the daugh*
	of Prince Frederick Henry of Orange.) G. HONTHORST, 1(
	A Child Gathering Pears.
	Portraits of Frederick William I. of Brandenbourg, and
	Wife, Louisa Henrietta of Nassau. (*From the Mauritsh*.
LONDON.	
Stafford House.	Christ before Caiaphas.
Buckingham Pal:	The Duke and Duchess of Buckingham and Children.
MADRID. *Gall:*	The Incredulity of St. Thomas.
MUNICH. *Pina-*	The Deliverance of St. Peter.
kothek.	Ceres Transforming the Peasant into a Lizard.
	The Roman Charity.
	The Prodigal Son. GERART VAN HONTHORST, FECIT, 162:
	Christ Teaching in the Temple.
	The Prodigal Son.

s. *Louvre.* Pilate Washing his Hands. (*Engraved in London.*)
Concert. G. HONTHORST. FE. 1624.
Triumph of Silenus.
Portrait of Charles Louis, Count Palatine of the Rhine.
G. HONTHORST, 1640.
Portrait of Prince Rupert.
The Lute-player. G. HONTHORST. F. 1614.
A Young Shepherd.

II. *Gallery.* An Old Man Reading.

ERDAM. A Soldier Lighting his Pipe.

Museum. Head of an Old Man.—(1647 *and with monogram.*)

ETERSBURG. Christ before Caiaphas. (*Called "Christ before Pilate" in the*
Hermitage. *catalogue.*)
The Concert.
Portrait of Charles Louis, Count Palatine of the Rhine.
Painted in England.
Portrait of Rupert, Count Palatine of the Rhine. *Painted*
in England.
Portrait of a Man with a Glass and a Violin.
Portrait of a Young Woman Playing the Mandolin and
Singing.
Portrait of a Woman with a Spinning-wheel.
Portrait of Young Woman, Singeing her Hair.
Portrait of an Old Woman, Praying.

ε. *Borghese P.* Lot and his Daughters.

NA. *Belvedere.* Christ before Pilate.
A Boy Teasing a Dog.
St. Jerome.

URN ABBEY. Portrait of the Countess of Bedford.

ADRIAEN BROUWER.

.ℬ

ERDAM. A Village Revel.

Museum. Peasants Fighting. (*More like a work of Joos van Cracsbeeck.*)

.IN. *Museum.* The Toilet. *Engraved in the Series of "The Seven Sins" as*
"Superbia."

BERLIN. *Museum.* A Moon-lit Landscape.
 A Dance of Peasants. (*Doubted.*)
 The Smoker. (*Perhaps by David Ryckaert, the younger.*)
 The Smoker. (*Perhaps by Joos van Craesbeeck.*)
 [*All five of the above came from the Suermondt Collecti*
 and are given as doubted in the Official Catalogue.]
BRUSSELS. *Mus:* A Fight in a Cabaret.
 Arenberg Coll: Interior of a Tavern.
CASSEL. *Gallery.* Peasants Playing Cards.
 Peasants in an Ale-house.
DRESDEN. *Gall:* Two Peasants Fighting.
 Two Peasants Sitting at a Table.
 A Caricature. (*A study.*)
 A Caricature.
 A Peasant with a Child.
DULWICH. *Gall:* Interior of an Ale-house.
FLORENCE. *Uffizi.* Peasants Drinking in a Tavern.
 The Topers.
FRANKFORT. A Peasant doctoring the foot of another Peasant. *Etched*
 Städel. J. *Eissenhardt.*
 A Peasant having his back doctored. A. B. *Etched by*
 Eissenhardt.
 A Man Taking Medicine. A. B. *Etched by J. Eissenhardt.*
LONDON. *Bridge-*
 water House. Peasants Singing.
 Hertford Coll: A Sleeping Peasant.
MADRID. *Mus:* The Comic Trio.
 Music in the Kitchen.
 The Conversation.
MUNICH. *Pina-* Peasants Playing Cards.
 kothek. Spanish Soldiers Playing at Dice.
 Three Peasants smoking.
 A Peasant Playing the Fiddle while others sing.
 Two Peasants Fighting separated by a third.
 Peasants Fighting in an Ale-house.
 A Village Doctor Dressing a Peasant's Arm.
 Peasants Singing.
 A Peasant with a Lame Foot.
PARIS. *Louvre.* Interior of a Smoking-room.
 The Smoker. (*Engraved by Gaujean.*)
PESTH. *Gallery.* Peasants Drinking.

ii. *Gallery.*   Three Peasants Drinking.
'ETERSBURG.   The Drinker. (*With monogram.*)
Hermitage.   Peasants in an Ale-house.
                     Peasants Quarrelling.
                     The Flute-Player.
                     Interior of a Peasant's Cottage - *two men smoking and one
                         singing.*
:NA. *Belvedere.* A Peasant Sitting on a Cask with a Mug and Pipe.
Czernin Coll: Peasants.

GERARD TER-BORCH.

TERDAM.   Portrait of Gerard Ter-Borch.   (*With monogram.*)
Museum.   Portrait of his Wife.   (*With monogram.*)
                     Paternal Advice.   (*Similar pictures are in the Berlin Museum,
                         and in the Bridgewater House Gallery, London; and a
                         study for it in the Dresden Gallery.*)
                     The Treaty of Münster in 1648.   (*A copy of the picture in
                         the National Gallery, London.*)
Six Coll: The Duet.
                     A Girl Writing.
der Hoop C. A Boy and a Dog.
VERP. *Mus:* The Mandolin-player.
AN. *Museum.* Paternal Advice.   (*Engraved by J. G. Wille.*)
                     Portrait of Herr van Marienburg.
                     Portrait of Gertrud van Marienburg, *his wife, aunt of Gerard
                         Ter-Borch.* (*With monogram.*)
                     The Consultation.   G. T. BORCH, 1635.
                     Portrait of a Man.
                     Portrait of a Young Man.
                     The Smoker.
                     The Family of the Knife-grinder.   (*With monogram.*)
EL. *Gallery.* The Lute-player.
                     A Lady and Gentleman Playing.

COPENHAGEN.   Portraits of a Gentleman and his Wife.
        Gallery.   Portrait of a Lady.
DEVENTER. *Town*   Portraits of Twenty Members of the Town Council of Devent
        Hall.   1667.
DRESDEN.   The Trumpeter.   (*With monogram.*)
        Gallery.   A Lady in a Satin Gown Washing her Hands. G. T. BORCH
                    The Lute-player.   (*With monogram given above.*)
                    Paternal Advice.   (*Study for the Berlin Gallery Picture.*)
FLORENCE. *Uffizi.* A Dutch Lady.
FRANKFORT.   Portrait of a Lady. *With monogram.* (*In the Städel.*)
HAGUE. *Gallery.* The Message (or "The Trumpeter"). (*With monogram, a
                    date* 1655.) *Engraved by Audouin, Lerouge, Réveil, a
                    Zeelander, and lithographed by Last.*
                    Portrait of Gerard Ter-Borch. (*Lithographed by F.
                    Waanders.*)
Steengracht Coll: A Mother and Child.
LONDON. *Nation-* The Guitar Lesson.   (*Engraved in the Choiseul Gallery.*)
  al Gallery.   The Peace of Münster. G. T BORCH, F. MONASTERII, A. 16.
                    (*Engraved by Jonas Suijderhoef.*)
Ashburton Coll: A Musical Party.
Bridgewater Ho: Paternal Advice.
Buckingham Pal: A Girl Reading a Letter to her Mother.
  Eastlake Coll: Portrait of a Gentleman.
LYONS. *Museum.*   The Messenger.
MONTPELLIER   A Girl Seated Pouring out Wine. (*In the Musée Fabre.*)
MUNICH. *Pina-*   Interior of Peasant's Cottage.
        kothek.   A Boy with a Dog. (*With monogram.*)
                    A Trumpeter Bringing a Letter to a Lady. G. T. BORCH.
PARIS. *Louvre.* An Officer Offering Money to a Young Lady. (*With mon
                    gram.*) *Engraved by Audouin and in Filhol.*
                    The Music Lesson. BURG. F. 1660. (*Engraved by Mons a
                    Lavallée, and in Filhol.*)
                    The Concert.   T. BURG. (*Engraved in Filhol.*)
                    An Ecclesiastical Assembly.
ST. PETERSBURG.   A Cavalier presenting a Glass of Wine to a Young Lady.
  Hermitage.   An Old Jew with a Violin.
                    A Lady in a Satin Gown Standing Reading a Letter, j
                    presented to her by a Page.
                    A Lady in a Satin Gown Sits Reading a Letter, just p
                    sented by a Peasant.
                    The Musicians.

PETERSBURG. A Soldier Offers Money to a Servant-maid, who holds a Jug
  Hermitage.   and a Glass. (Signed.)
NNA. Belvedere. A Young Woman Peeling an Apple for a Child.
echtenstein C. Portraits of Herr van Marienburg and his Wife, Gertrud, aunt
               of Gerard Ter-Borch. (Portraits of these persons are also
               in the Berlin Gallery.)

ADRIAAN VAN OSTADE.

$$\mathcal{A}. \; O. \qquad \mathcal{A}^{\mathcal{O}}$$

STERDAM.   A Painter's Studio. A. V. O. (as above, i.e. left hand). Etched
  Museum.   by Unger and by L. Löwenstam.
            Travellers Resting. A. V. OSTADE, 1671. Etched by J. A.
              Boland.
            The Charlatan. A. V. OSTADE, 1648.
            The Baker. Etched by A. van Ostade.
'ix Collection. The Fish-wife.
 der Hoop C. Peasants round a Hearth. (Dated 1661.)
WERP. Mus: The Smoker. A. V. OSTADE, 1655.
LIN. Gallery. Portrait of an Old Woman. A. V. OSTADE, 16—
            ·The Lyre-player before an Ale-house. A. V. OSTADE, 1640.
            The Smoker. A. V. OSTADE, 1667.
NSWICK. Gall: Annunciation of the Birth of Christ.
            A Peasant Smoking.
SSELS. Gall: Man Eating Herrings. (Lithographed by Madou and by
              Fourmois.)
r.nberg Coll: Interior of a Tavern.
EL. Gallery. Peasants in an Arbour of an Ale-house. A. V. OSTADE, 1676.
            Peasants Drinking in an Alehouse. A. V. OSTADE, 16—.
            Peasants Playing Cards. A. V. OSTADE, 1659.
MSTADT. Gall: Peasants Dancing.
SDEN. Gall: Peasants in an Ale-house. A. V. OSTADE, 1639.
            The Painter's Studio. A. V. OSTADE, 1663.

DRESDEN. *Gall:* Two Peasants Eating at a Table. A. V. OSTADE, 1663.

Two Peasants before an Ale-house, one Lighting a Pipe. A. OSTADE, 1664.

Interior of an Ale-house, with Men and Women. A. OSTADE, 1679.

Peasants Playing Cards. AD. OSTADE, Ft.

DULWICH. *Gall:* Boors Making Merry. A. V. OSTADE, 164—

Man and Woman in Conversation.

A Man Smoking. A. V. OSTADE.

A Woman with a Jug. A. V. OSTADE.

FLORENCE. *Uffizi.* A Man at a Window.

FRANKFORT. Interior of a Shed. A. V. OSTADE, 1656. (*In the Städel.*)

HAGUE. *Gallery.* Peasants in an Inn. A. V. OSTADE, 1662. (*Engraved Bovinet, Chataigner, Bemme, C. C. A. Last, and by A. Zeelander.*)

The Fiddler. A. V. OSTADE, 1673. (*Engraved by Ch aigner, Bovinet, Boutrois, and by A. L. Zeelander, a lithographed by C. C. Last and by J. J. Mesker. Ploos v Amstel made a fac-simile engraving from a drawing by van Ostade, dated 1673, exactly similar to this painting.*)

LONDON. *Nat: Gal:* The Alchymist. A. V. OSTADE, 1661.

Apsley House. A Company of Peasants. (*The drawing for this picture is the British Museum.*)

Ashburton Coll: Peasants Playing and Singing. (*Dated* 1661.)

A Village Scene. (*Dated* 1676.)

Bridgewater Ho: Peasants Playing Skittles. A. V. OSTADE, 1676.

Portrait of an Old Man, *probably a lawyer,* 1671.

Buckingham Pal: Peasants Conversing. A. V. OSTADE, 1650.

An Interior, with Peasants Smoking. A. V. OSTADE, 1665.

Northbrook Coll: Four Persons Playing at Cards. (*Dated* 1648.)

MADRID. *Gallery..* A Concert.

Peasants Feeding.

A Toper.

MUNICH. *Pina-lothek.* Interior of a Peasant's Cottage. A. V. OSTADE, 1647.

Peasants Quarrelling. A. V. OSTADE, 1656.

Peasants Playing and Dancing. A. V. OSTADE, 1647.

A Toper. A. V. OSTADE.

Peasants Carousing. A. V. OSTADE.

Peasants in an Ale-house. A. V. OSTADE, 16—.

Peasants in an Ale-house, with a Woman and her Children.

PARIS. *Louvre.* The Family of Adriaan van Ostade. (*Engraved in Filhol.*)

Louvre. The School-master. A. V. OSTADE, 1662. *(Engraved by Bovinet, and in London.)*
The Fish-market. *(Engraved by Claessens and in Filhol.)*
Interior of a Cottage. A. V. OSTADE, 1642.
A Man Reading in his Cabinet.
A Smoker. *(Engraved by Dupréel and in Filhol.)*
A Toper. A. V. OSTADE, 1668. *(Engraved by David, as " Le Vieillard Joyeux," and in Filhol.)*

Gallery. Interior of a Peasant's Cottage. A. V. OSTADE.
Interior, with Peasants.
Peasants Drinking.
Interior, with Peasants.
A Man Mending a Pen.
Interior, with Peasants. A. V. OSTADE.

DAM. *Mus:* A Man Reading. A. V. OSTADE.
A Village Tavern.

ERSBURG. A Village Fête.

'ermitage. A Peasant Family.
The Violin-player. *(Signed and dated 1648.)*
An Old Woman Seated on a Window-sill, surrounded by a Vine.
A Village Minstrel playing a Hurdy-gurdy.
The Baker. *(Signed.)*
The Village Concert.
Peasants Smoking.
Peasants, while Smoking and Drinking, listen to a Woman who Reads a Letter.
A Peasant Family.
Peasants in an Ale-house.
The Touch. *(Signed.)*
The Sight. *(Signed and dated 1651.)*
The Taste.
Peasant in a Cottage.
Landscape.

.. Czernin Peasants.

'ollection. A Smoker.
A Drinker.

FERDINAND BOL.

AMSTERDAM.	Portrait of Ferdinand Bol. (*In a carved, wooden, ornam*
Museum.	*frame of the same date as the picture.*)
	Portrait of Arthur Quellinus, *Sculptor.* BOL, 1663.
	Portrait of Admiral Michiel Adriaansz de Ruijter. F.
	FECIT, 1677. (*Engraved by W. van Senus and etch*
	J. A. Boland.)
	A Mother with her two Children. F. BOL FECIT. (*For*
	over a chimney-piece in the house which is known as the
	penhuis, and which at present contains the picture gal
	it probably represents members of the Trip Family.)
	The Instruction. F. BOL, 1663. (*Formerly over a chi*
	piece in the house which at present contains the p
	gallery : it probably represents members of the Trip Fan
Town Hall.	Four Regents of the Leprosy Hospital.
Van der Hoop C.	Portrait of Admiral de Ruijter.
BERLIN. *Museum.*	Portrait of an Old Lady. F. BOL FECIT, 1642.
BRUNSWICK. *Gall:*	Portrait of a Man.
BRUSSELS. *Gall:*	Portrait of a Man. F. BOL F. 1660. *The F and the B*
	laced as given above. (*Formerly called a Rembrandt.*)
	Portrait of a Woman. F. BOL F. 1660. (*Formerly cal*
	Rembrandt.)
	Portrait of Saskia van Ulenburgh, *wife of Rembrandt*
	Rijn.
	A Philosopher in Meditation. (*A somewhat similar p*
	is in the Louvre.)
CAMBRIDGE.	A Portrait. (*In the Fitzwilliam Museum.*)
COPENHAGEN.	The Holy Sepulchre. F. BOL FECIT, 1644.
Gallery.	Portrait of a Lady. F. BOL, 1656.
	Portrait of Admiral de Ruijter. F. BOL, 1668.
DRESDEN. *Gall:*	Rest on the Flight into Egypt. F. BOL FECIT, 1644.
	Jacob's Vision. F. BOL FECIT.
	Joseph Presenting Jacob to Pharaoh.
	Portrait of Ferdinand Bol.

N. *Gall:* David's Charge to Solomon. (*Dated* 1643.)
:FORT. Portrait of a Young Man holding his Hat and Gloves in his
Städel. Hand. F. BOL, 1644. (*Etched by Eissenhardt.*)
Portrait of a Man with Curly Hair. F. BOL, 1659.
3. *Gallery.* Portrait of Michiel Adriaansz de Ruijter. (*Lithographed by Elink Sterk.*)
Portrait of Engel de Ruijter. F. BOL, 1669. (*Lithographed by J. H. Weissenbruch.*)
POOL. The Angel appearing to Hagar. (*In the Institute.*)
N. *Nat:Gal:* Portrait of an Astronomer. F. BOL FECIT, 1652.
rook Coll: Portraits of a Bride and Bridegroom.
A Scene from Guarini's " Pastor Fido."
:N. *Town H.* Allegory of Peace. (*Painted in* 1664.)
:H. *Pina-* Abraham, about to Offer up Isaac, stopped by an Angel.
kothek. Portrait of a Man Clothed in Black.
. *Louvre.* A Philosopher in Meditation.
A Young Prince of Holland in a Chariot drawn by Goats
F. BOL, 1654.
Portrait of a Mathematician. (*Engraved by Klaubert and by Wavmans.*)
Portrait of a Man. F. BOL, 1659.
. *Gallery.* Portrait of a Man.
:RDAM. *Mus:* Portrait of Dirk van der Waeijen. F. BOL, 1656.
Portrait of a Lady. F. BOL FECIT, 1652.
:TERSBURG. Portrait of a Countess of Nassau-Siegen. (*Probably Ernestina, wife of John, the younger, of Nassau-Siegen.*)
Hermitage.
Portraits of Persons, unknown—as Theseus and Ariadne.
The Savant, writing.
Portrait of a Man, *turning over the leaves of a book by his side.*
Portrait of a Lady, *in black, seated, holding her gloves.*
Portrait of a Young Man, *his right hand on a table.*
Portrait of a Young Lady, *standing before an old man, who is seated.* (*Miscalled " Esther and Ahasuerus."*)
The Philosopher. (*Signed.*)
Portrait of a Young Man. (*Signed and dated* 1641.)
Portrait of an Old Woman, *seated, with a book on her knees. Signed and dated* 1651. OUT 81 JAER (*formerly in the Collection of the Duke of Portland.*)

BARTHOLOMEUS VAN DER HELST.

AMSTERDAM.
Museum.

The Banqnet of the Civic Guard ("De Schutters-maaltij BARTHOLOMEUS VAN DER HELST FECIT A°., 1648. (*Engr by Patas and by J. W. Kaiser ; and lithographed by Loo.*)

The Syndics of the Confraternity of St. Sebastian at sterdam. BARTHOLOMEUS VANDER HELST, 1657.

Portrait of Lieutenant-Admiral Aart van Nes. B. VAN HELST, 1668. (*In the background is a Naval Co painted by Ludolf Backhuisen.*)

Portrait of Geertruida den Dubbelde, wife of Aart van B. VAN DER HELST, 1668.

Portrait of Maria Henrietta Stuart, widow of William II

Portrait of a Man, in black.

Portrait of a Woman. B. V. H.

Portrait of Vice-Admiral Egbert Meeuwiszoon Korte (*Engraved by A. Blateling.*)

Portrait of Andries Bicker, Burgomaster of Amster B. VAN DER HELST, 1642. (*Engraved by J. v. Vils and J. Houbraken.*)

Portrait of Gerdrard Bicker, Anieszoon, "Bailli' Muiden.

Town Hall.

Members of the Archery Guild of Amsterdam. (*Paint 1639.*)

Four Members of the Archery Guild, with the Steward a Boy. (*Painted in 1656.*)

Six Collection. Van der Helst at table with his wife Constantia Reijnst.

ANTWERP. *Mus:* Portrait of a Young Girl, as Diana.

BERLIN. *Mus:* Portrait of an Old Woman.

BRUSSELS. *Gall:* Portrait of Himself. B. VANDER HELST, 1664.

Portrait of a Woman, *said to be his Wife, Constantia Rei* B. VANDER HELST, 1664.

CASSEL. *Gall:* Portrait of a Man (*three-quarter length*). B. V. DER H 1642.

COPENHAGEN. Portrait of a Man. B. VAN DER HELST, 1651.

Gallery. Portrait of a Man. B. VAN HELST.

DEN. *Gall:* Portrait of a Woman, who Draws back a Curtain. B. VAN DER HELST, 1654.

Portrait of a Man, Holding his Cloak in his Left Hand.

Portrait of an Old Woman, with a White Cap.

Portrait of the Wife of Andries Bicker, of Amsterdam. B. VAN DER HELST, 1642. ÆTA 48.

ENCE. *Uffizi.* Portrait of Himself.

Pitti Pal: Portrait of a Man.

KFORT.

Städel. Portrait of a Woman. B. VAN DER HELST, 1656

BURGH. Portrait of a Man. (*In the National Gallery.*)

E. *Gallery.* Portrait of Paulus Potter. B. VAN DER HELST, 1654. (*Engraved by F. L. Huijgens; lithographed by J. C. d' Arnaud Gerkens.*)

PTON COURT. Portrait of a Dutchman.

. *Gallery.* Portraits.

ON. *National Gallery.* Portrait of a Lady, Standing (*half-length*).

Hertford Ho: Family Portrait.

sdowne Ho: Bust Portrait of a Lady. B. VAN DER HELST, 1640.

hbrook Coll: Portrait of an Officer.

CH. *Pinakothek.* Portrait of Admiral Martin Harperts Tromp.

Portrait of a Man, in a Black Dress, Holding his Gloves in his Left Hand and his Cap in his Right.

Portrait of a Lady, Holding a Fan in her Right Hand.

. *Louvre.* The Syndics of the Confraternity of St. Sebastian ("*Le Jugement du prix de l'arc.*") BARTHOLOMEUS VAN DER HELST, 1653. (*Engraved by Hulmer, and in Filhol.*) *A sketch for the picture in Amsterdam Museum.*

Portrait of a Man (half-length).

Portrait of a Lady. VAN DER HELST, 1655.

A. *Gallery.* Portrait of a Man.

ERDAM. A Cavalier and a Lady in a Park (*the landscape by A. van Everdingen*). B. VAN DER HELST FECIT, 1654.

Museum. Portrait of a Preacher. B. VAN DER HELST, F. 1638.

Portrait of Daniel Bernard. (*Signed and dated* 1669.)

ETERSBURG. The New Market, Amsterdam. (*Signed and dated* 1669.)

Hermitage. The Presentation of the *Fiancée*. (*Signed and dated* 1647.)

A Family Group, *of five persons.*

A Family Group: *a Cavalier with his wife and child.*

Portrait of Govaert Fliuck.

St. Petersburg.   Portrait of a Lady, *in a black dress.*
Hermitage.   Portrait of a Man, *seated, tying his garter.* (*Signed and*
                       1670.)
                    Portrait of a Young Lady, *in a red dress.*
                    Portrait of a Man, *in red.*
                    Portrait of a Man, *in black.*

GERARD DOU.

GD

Amsterdam.   Portrait of Himself. G. DOU. (*Engraved by Schouman.*)
Museum.   Evening School. G. DOU. (*Etched by J A. Boland, and*
                       graphed by Van Loo.)
                    The Hermit.
                    Curiosity.
                    Portraits of Pieter van der Werf, Burgomaster of Le
                       and his Wife. BERCHEM G. DOU. *The G and the D*
                       laced as given above. (*The portraits are by Dou, the*
                       scape by Berchem.)
Six Coll :   The Dentist.
                    A Girl at a Window. G. DOU, 1667.
                    A Candle-light Effect.
Van der Hoop C.   Fish-woman.
Berlin. *Museum.*   The Penitent Magdalen. G. DOU, 1656.
                    Portrait of an Old Woman. G. DOU.
                    The Store-room.
Brunswick. *G.*   Portrait of Himself.
Brussels. *Gall:*   Portrait of Himself. G. DOU.
Arenberg Coll :   An Old Woman Sitting at a Table, covered with Gold.
Cassel. *Gallery.* Bust Portrait of an Old Man, with a blue feather in his
                    Bust Portrait of a Woman.
Copenhagen.   The Doctor. G. DOU.
Gallery.   Girl with a Light. G. DOU, 165(8 ?).
Dresden. *Gallery.* Portrait of Himself. G. DOU, 1647.
                    A Grey Cat on a Window-sill ; in the background,
                       before his easel. G. DOU, 1657.

PEN. *Gall:* A Girl Plucking Grapes at a Window. G. DOU, 1658.

Gerard Dou Playing the Violin. G. DOU, 1665. (*See frontispiece.*)

A School-master Mending his Pen. G. DOU, 1671.

The Dentist, with a Boy, whose tooth he has just extracted. G. DOU, 1672.

A Hermit Praying. G. DOU.

A Girl Watering a Plant. G. DOU.

Still Life. G. DOU.

A Girl Sitting at a Table.

Portrait of Gerard Dou's Mother, reading the newspaper.

An Old Woman Searching for her Lost Thread.

A Girl in Wine-cellar.

Portrait of Gerard Dou's Mother, reading a book.

An Old Woman Reading a Book.

A Young Man and a Girl.

VICH *Gall:* A Lady Playing on the Virginals.

ENCE. *Uffizi.* Portrait of Himself. G. DOU, 1618.

A School-master. G. DOU.

The Pan-cake Seller.

!KFORT. A Girl Preparing Supper. (*In the Städel*).

JR. *Gallery.* The Young Tailoress (or, "The Young Mother"). G. DOU, 1658. (*Engraved by Réveil, as "La Jeune Mère;" by Chataigner, as "La Jeune Ménagère"; and by A. L. Zeelander; and lithographed by C. C. A. Last.*)

A Young Woman Holding a Lamp. (*Engraved by J. F. Lange; and lithographed by C. C. A. Last; and by A. C. Nunnink, in reverse.*)

ION. *National Gallery.* Portrait of Himself. G. DOU F.

The Poulterer's Shop. G. DOU. (*Engraved in the "Choiseul Gallery."*)

Portrait of Dou's Wife. G. DOU.

ingham Pal: An Old Man.

A Kitchen-maid. G. DOU, 1646.

A Mother Nursing a Child.

water Ho: The Violin-player. G. DOU, 1637.

Portrait of Himself.

hbrook Coll: A Lady Playing the Spinet.

IPELLIER. The Mouse-trap. (*In the Musée Fabre.*)

ICH. *Pinakothek.* An Old Woman Looking Through a Window. G. DOU.

Portrait of an Old Painter in his Studio (*said to be Jurian or Georg Ovens.*) G. DOU, 1649.

MUNICH. *Pina-*   A Beggar asking Alms of an Old Woman Selling Vegetabl
   kothek.   The Bakeress.
        Portrait of Himself. G. DOU, 1663. Aet 56.
        A Lady's-maid Curling her Mistress's Hair.
        An Old Woman Combing a Boy's Hair. G. DOU.
        A Hermit Praying. G. DOU. G. D., 1670.
        A Hermit Reading. G. DOU. (*A late work.*)
        The Charlatan. G. DOU, 1652. (*Containing portrait*
          Gerard Dou and some of his relations.)
        A Spinner Saying Grace before Dining. G. DOU.
        The Herring-seller. G. DOV., 1667.
        A Maid-servant Emptying a Brass Can out of a Window.
        An Old Woman Cutting Bread for the Supper of Herself
          Two Children.
        A Young Girl with a Light in one Hand and a Lanter
          the other Looking out of a Window. G. DOU, 1658.
        A Hermit Praying.

PARIS. *Louvre*.   The Woman with the Dropsy 1663, G. DOU. OVT 65 J
         (*Engraved by Claessins, by Fosseyeux, and in Filhol.*)
        A Silver Ewer and Salver. G. DOU. (*Painted on the sh*
        of an ebony box which formerly contained the painting of '
          Woman with the Dropsy.")
        The Village Grocer. 1647, G. DOU. (*Engraved in Filho*
        The Trumpeter. G. DOU. (*Engraved in Filhol.*)
        The Dutch Cook. (*Engraved by P. E. Moitte; in mez*
        by Sarabat, and by Lips.)
        A Woman Hanging up a Cock at a Window. G. DOU,]
        (*Engraved by Géraut, and in Filhol.*)
        The Gold-weigher. G. DOU, 1664.
        The Dentist. (*Engraved by Kesler.*)
        Reading the Bible. (*Engraved by Defrey, and in Fi*
        The old man and woman represented are said to be por
        of Gerard Dou's father and mother.
        Portrait of Himself, at a Window Holding his Palette
          Brushes. (*Engraved by Oortman and in Filhol.*) G. D
        Portrait of an Old Woman, *Reading at a Table.* G. DOU.
        graved in Filhol.)

PESTH. *Gallery*.   St. Anthony, the Hermit.
ST. PETERSBURG.   A Doctor and an Old Woman. (*Signed.*)
   Hermitage.   The Herring-seller—*a boy buying a herring of an old Wo*
        (*Signed.*)

PETERSBURG.   Portrait of Gerard Dou.   (*Signed and dated* **1665.**)
Hermitage.   Portrait of an Old Man, *reading.*   (*Signed.*)
A Monk, *seated reading.*
An Old Woman Winding Thread.
A Young Peasant Woman Preparing to Bathe.
A Man Preparing to Bathe.
A Young Woman Combing her Hair by the side of a River.
(*Signed.*)
An Old Woman Reading.   (*Signed.*)
Portrait of a Man, with a Broad-brimmed Hat.   (*Signed.*)

:NNA.   *Belve-*   The Doctor and an Old Woman.   (*Painted in* 1653.)
dere.   An Old Woman Watering Flowers at a Window.
Czernin Coll :   Portrait of Gerard Dou.
A Party Playing at Cards.
iechtenstein C.   Portrait of Gerard Dou.
RDOUR CASTLE.   The Blind Tobit going to Meet his Son.

PHILIPS WOUWERMAN.

STERDAM.   A Combat of Peasants.
Museum.   The Riding-school.
The Farrier.   (*The right hand monogram.*)
Landscape.   (*The left hand monogram.*)
Stag Hunt.
A Hawking Party.
The Victorious Peasants.
The Restive White Horse.
An Encampment.
[*All of the above works bear the painter's monogram.*]
The Watering-place.
ix Collection.   Landscape.

Six Collection.	Stable.
	Landscape.
Van der Hoop C.	Landscape. (*Part by Ruisdael.*)
ANTWERP. *Mus:*	Halt of Cavaliers. (*With monogram.*)
	Halt of Cavaliers. (*With monogram.*)
BERLIN. *Mus:*	The Riding-School. (*With monogram.*) " *A good work the best time of the artist.*"
.	Halt of a Hunting Party by a Stream. (*With monogram.*)
	A Hunting Party Setting Out.
	Horses at a Forge.
	Winter Landscape.
	The Hay-waggon.
BRUSSELS. *Gall:*	Departure for the Hunt. (*With monogram.*)
	A Hunting Party. (*With monogram.*)
CASSEL. *Gall:*	A Riding School.
	Departure for the Hunt.
	A Harbour.
	Landscape.
	A Sea Piece—*Persons Buying and Selling Fish.*
	A Fight between Europeans, and Moors and Turks.
	A Stable.
	Peasants Taken Prisoners by Soldiers.
	A Hawking Party.
	The Forge.
	And thirteen others [these works, twenty-three in all, are sig with the painter's monogram].
COPENHAGEN.	A Hunting Party. (*With monogram.*)
Gallery.	Travellers at an Inn. (*With monogram.*)
DRESDEN. *Gall:*	Landscape, with Houses and Trees.
	Corn field.
	Hawking Party.
	Return from Hunting.
	A Man Driving a Cart before an Inn.
	The Annunciation to the Shepherds.
	John the Baptist Preaching.
	Stag-hunt.
	[The above are in his early manner.]
	Hawking Party.
	Landscape, with Gibbet.
	A Peasant Watering his Horse.
	A Family Reposing.

RESDEN. *Gall :* Cavaliers Stopping before a Forge.

Leaving the Inn. 1649.

Combat of Cavalry and Infantry.

[*The above are in his second manner.*]

Hawking Party Setting Out.

A Horse Fair.

Travellers Stopping before an Inn.

A House by the side of a River—*a Cavalier Riding by.*

A Cavalier having his Horse Shod.

Hawking.

Cavaliers Drinking.

Fishermen with their Nets full of Fish, on the Sea-shore.

A Horse being Shod. (*Signed* P. W. ; *perhaps by Pieter Wouwerman. Engraved by Moyreau as " Le travail du maréchal."*)

Ruins on the Bank of a River.

Combat on a Bridge. (*A fine work.*)

Departure for the Chase.

Return from the Chase.

Combat of Cavalry near a Castle Defended by Artillery.

[*The above are in his best manner*].

A Capuchin Distributing Alms. (*Highly finished. Engraved by Moyreau as " L'Aumône des Capucins."*)

A Cavalier's Horse Rearing in Passing a Cart. (*Engraved by Le Bas as " Le Pot au lait."*

Combat between Peasants and Cavalry. (*Engraved by Moyreau as " Le Pillage des Reiters."*)

Horse Fair.

Cavalry Combat near a Mill. (*Engraved by Moyreau as " L'Embrasement du moulin."*)

A Stable of an Inn—Travellers Starting. (*A masterpiece.*)

Landscape, with a Waterfall. (*Highly finished. Engraved by Moyreau as " La Cascade."*)

Departure for the Chase.

A Bear and Wild-boars Attacked by Hunters. (*Engraved by Le Bas.*)

A Horse being Shod. (*Engraved by Moyreau as "La Grotte du maréchal."*)

The Ford.

The Halt.

Landscape with a Lake, and Stag-hunt.

DRESDEN. *Gall:* A Camp by a Wide River. (*From the Carignan Collection where it was known as the "Quartier général de l'armé hollandaise."*)

Combat between Germans and Turkish Cavalry.

[*The above, though of a little later period than the last mentioned group, are in the painter's best style, and ar many of them masterpieces.*]

A Cavalier Conversing with Fishermen.

A Peasant Watering his Horse.

Fishermen Drawing in their Nets.

Two Cavaliers Fighting with Pistols.

· [*The above are in a later manner. There are no less tha sixty-six works recorded under the name of Wouwerma. in this gallery ; of these about sixty are considere genuine ; they bear, with few exceptions, the monogram of the painter. They are arranged in chronological orde: so far as possible, and indicate the various stages of th growth of Wouwerman's art.*]

DULWICH *Gall:* A Halt of Sportsmen. (*With monogram.*)

Selling Fish on the Coast of Scheveningen. (*With mono gram.*)

A Halt of Travellers. (*With monogram.*)

A Halt of Three Cavaliers at a Way-side Inn. (*With mone gram.*)

Two Riders near a Fountain. (*Painted in his best period.*)

Peasants in the Fields. (*With monogram.*) *Engraved by R Cockburn.*

The Return from Hawking. (*With monogram.*) *Engraved b R. Cockburn and Moyreau.*

A Courtyard, with a Farrier. (*With monogram.*) *Engrave by R. Cockburn and Moyreau.*

The Halt of a Hunting Party. (*With monogram.*) *Engrave by Dequeranviller and Moyreau.*

FLORENCE. *Uffizi.* Huntsmen Resting.

FRANKFORT. A Halt of Horsemen before an Ale-house. (*Engraved b
  Städel. Moyreau.*)

A Halt of Two Cavaliers.

A Peasant Harnessing a Horse.

A Stable with Three Horses.

A Landscape, with a Cavalier and a Lady.

[*All bear the monogram of the painter.*]

IAGUE, *Gallery.* The Arrival at the Inn. (*Engraved by Fuchs and lithographed by Craeijvanger.*)

The Departure from the Inn. (*Lithographed by Last.*)

Halt of Huntsmen. (*Engraved by Wachsmuth.*)

A Cavalier Riding a Horse in a Park. (*Engraved by J. Moyreau ; Zeelander, and Desaulx ; and lithographed by C. C. A. Last.*)

The Ford (the Hay-cart). (*Engraved by Duplessis-Bertaux, by Dupréel, by Huijgens ; and lithographed by Craeijvanger.*)

A Battle. [*The composition of this picture is similar to that of the work known as the " Battle of Nördlingen," in the Pina-kothek (Munich, Cab : xiv. 428).*] Engraved by Huijgens, and lithographed by Last.

A Camp. (*Lithographed by Last.*)

Huntsmen Resting. (*Engraved by Niquet, and in reverse by Niquet " the younger."*)

[*All the above bear the painter's monogram.*]

teengracht Coll : Landscape, with Figures.

ONDON. *National Gallery.* Halt of Officers.

Interior of a Stable.

On the Sea Shore.

Gathering Faggots.

Landscape.

The Stag-hunt.

A Battle—Cavalry and Infantry.

[*All with the monogram.*]

A Landscape with Two Figures. (*Henderson Bequest.*)

Apsley House. Return from the Chase. (*With monogram.*)

Ashburton Coll : The Pigeon-house.

uckingham Pal : Horse Fair. (*With monogram.*)   .

Horseman and Lady before a Tavern.

" Le Coup de Pistolet."

ridgewater Ho : Battle of Cavalry. (*With monogram.*)

Dudley House. The Attack. (*With monogram.*)

orthbrook Coll : Horsemen near a River.

LADRID. *Mus :* A Huntsman Halting.

The Two Horses.

Starting for the Hunt.

A Hunting Party.

Hunters Fording a River.

Hunters in a Park near a Fountain.

Leaving the Inn.

MADRID.   *Gall:*   The Halt at an Inn.
                    Fight between Cavalry and Infantry.
                    Lancers and Infantry Fighting.
MUNICH.   A Stag-hunt.
      Pinakothek. A Horseman Crossing a Bridge.
                    Travellers Nearing a Stream.
                    A Stable (c. 397).
                    Waggoners Stopping by a River.
                    A Stable (c. 403).
                    A Driver Watering his Horse.
                    Horses being Ridden to Drink.
                    Training a Horse.
                    A Winter Landscape, *with Skaters.*
                    The Battle of Nördlingen. 6 Sept., 1634.
                    Huntsmen and Ladies Resting after the Chase by a Statue of Pai
                    Soldiers Plundering a Village. (*The pendant, the " Victorio*
                        Peasants," is in the Museum, Amsterdam.)
                    The Departure from the Camp.
                        [*The above, with few exceptions, bear the painter's monogran*
                            There are other works, with less claim to genuineness, i
                            this gallery, given to Wouwerman.]
PARIS.   *Louvre.* The Fat Ox. (*With monogram.*)
                    The Wooden Bridge over the Torrent. (*With monogram.*)
                    Departure for the Chase (No. 567). *With monogram.*)
                    Departure for the Chase (No. 568). (*Engraved by Moyreau.*)
                    The Stag-hunt. (*Engraved by Daudet and by Moyreau, an*
                        in Filhol and Landon.)
                    The Riding-school. (*Engraved by Laurent, and in Filhol an*
                        Landon.)
                    Interior of a Stable.   (*Engraved by Moyreau, and in Filhol.*
                    A Cavalry Encounter.   (*With monogram.*)   *Engraved l*
                        Dupréel, and in Filhol and Landon.
                    Cavalry Attacking a Fort. (*With monogram.*)
                    Halt of Cavaliers before an Inn. (*With monogram.*)   *Fo*
                        merly ascribed to Pieter Wouwerman.
                    Cavaliers Halting near a Tent.
                    Halt of Soldiers.
                    The Hay-waggon.
PESTH.   *Gallery.* A Horse-dealer.
                    Watering Horses. (*Signed.*)
                    Landscape, with Mountains. (*Signed.*)

OTTERDAM.	A Rider on a White Horse. (*With monogram.*)
Museum.	A Cavalier on a Grey Horse.
г. PETERSBURG.	The Cat-hunt. (*Signed.*)
Hermitage.	A Riding Party. (*Four pictures of this subject.*)
	A Stable.
	The Ford. (*Signed.*)
	A Halt before an Inn. (*Nine pictures of this subject.*)
	A Forge.
	The Burning Mill. (*Signed.*)
	Combat of Cavalry. (*Signed.*)
	Combat between Poles and Turkish Cavalry. (*Signed, and dated* 1656.)
	Combat between Poles and Swedes.
	Travellers Watering their Horses.
	The Tent of the Vivandière. (*Signed.*)
	Hawking Party. (*Five pictures of this subject.*)
	The Stag-hunt. (*One of his best works.*)
	Interior of a Cabaret.
	A Winter Scene.
	Landscapes, with Figures. (*Signed.*)
VIENNA. *Academy.*	Landscape, with Animals.
Belvedere.	Landscape, with Reapers.
	Landscape, with an Attack of Robbers.
	Mountain Pass, with Robbers.
	Huntsmen Halting.
	Horses being Ridden to Drink.

ISACK VAN OSTADE.

AMSTERDAM.	A Village Inn. ISACK VAN OSTADE.
Museum.	The Merry Peasant.
Van der Hoop C.	A Way-side Inn.
ANTWERP. *Mus:*	Winter Landscape. ISACK VAN OSTADE, 1645.
BERLIN. *Mus:*	A Halt before an Inn. I. VAN OSTADE.
	Interior of a Dutch Peasant's Cottage. ISACK VAN OSTADE.
	A Peasant in a Flap-hat. ISACK VAN OSTADE.
BRUSSELS. *Mus:*	Travellers Halting. I. VAN OSTADE, 1660 (*sic.*). [*This date must be a forgery, for the painter was dead in* 1660.]
	Woman Winding Thread. OSTADE. P. (*Engraved by Laudet.*)
COPENHAGEN. *G.*	Winter Landscape, with Figures. ISACK OSTADE.

DRESDEN. *Gall:* Winter Landscape, with Figures. ISACK VAN OSTADE.
          Peasants Drinking and Dancing. I. VAN OSTADE.
LONDON. *Nation-* Village Scene. (*Engraved by Dunker.*)
al Gallery. Frost Scene. ISAAC VAN OSTADE.
          A Frozen River. I. V. OSTADE.
Ashburton Coll: Travellers and Villagers before an Inn.
Bridgewater Ho: A Village Street.
Buckingham Pal: Boors Making Merry. ISACK VAN OSTADE, 1646.
          A Village Street. ISACK VAN OSTADE, 1643.
Dudley House. Selling Fish. ISACK VAN OSTADE, 1649.
Lansdowne Ho: The Frozen Canal. ISACK VAN OSTADE.
Northbrook Coll: Winter Landscape.
MADRID. *Gallery.* Peasants.
MUNICH. *Pina-* Winter Landscape, with Skaters. ISAAK VAN OSTADE, 1644.
kothek. A Rocky Landscape, *with a Donkey and his Driver.* ISAC
          VAN OSTADE.
          Peasants Drinking. ISACK VAN OSTADE.
PARIS. *Louvre.* Travellers Halting at an Inn. ISACK VAN OSTADE.
          The Halt. (*Engraved in Filhol.*)
          A Frozen Canal, in Holland (No. 378). ISACK OSTADE. (*E*
          graved in Landon and Filhol.)
          A Frozen Canal, in Holland (No. 379). ISACK VAN OSTADE.
ROTTERDAM. *Mus:* A Village Scene. I. VAN OSTADE, 16—.
ST. PETERSBURG. A Winter Landscape, with Figures. (*Signed.*)
Hermitage. A Landscape—*Travellers Stopping before an Inn.* (*Signed.*)
          A Frozen Lake in Holland.
VIENNA. *Belvedere.* A Peasant having a Tooth Extracted.

JAN STEEN.

AMSTERDAM. *Mus:* His own Portrait. J. STEEN.
          The Fête of the Prince. J. STEEN. (*Etched by J. A. Boland.*)
          The Fête of St. Nicholas. J. STEEN. *The J and S inte-*
          laced as above. (*Engraved by Johannes de Marc; etched l*
          J. A. Boland.)
          The Parrot's Cage. J. STEEN. (*Engraved by Johannes <*
          Marc.)
          The Charlatan. J. STEEN.
          Village Wedding. J. STEEN, 1672.
          The Happy Return. J. STEEN. (*Etched by J. A. Boland.*)

DAM. *Mus:* The Baker Oostwaard, and his Wife, Catarina Keyzerswaard,
of Leyden. J. STEEN. (*Etched anonymously, and en-
graved by J. Bemme.*)

A Peasant Woman Cleaning a Pewter Pot. J. STEEN.

The Charlatan. J. STEEN.

The Libertine. J. STEEN.

en Coll : An Interior—*a man, with a herring and onions, and others.*
(*Engraved by Délignon.*)

ter Coll : The Rape of the Sabines.

yet Coll : " La Friandise."

six Coll : A Young Woman Eating Oysters. (*Engraved by Sluyter.*)

The Marriage (" Het Jodenbruidtjen "). J. STEEN, 1653.

no Coll : Peasants Fighting in an Ale-house.

· Bilt C : Ananias and Sapphira.

Hoop C. A Doctor and an Invalid Girl.

Interior—Drunken Peasants.

A Merry Company (" Soo de ouden songen, so pypen de
jonghen"). (*Signed, and dated* 1668.)

A Man and Woman Drinking.

A Merry Company.

v. Mus: Samson Insulted by the Philistines. J. STEEN.

The Village Wedding. J. STEEN.

:G. Gall : The Village Poet.

x. Gail : The Inn Garden. J. STEEN.

Players Quarrelling. J. S.

Dissolute Company.

ICK. The Signing of the Marriage Contract. (*Engraved by Baequoy.*)

Gallery. A Merry Company.

The Serenade.

3. Gall : The Rhetoricians. J. STEEN.

The Operator. J. STEEN.

The Bean Feast.

The Gallant Offer. J. STEEN. (*Engraved by Délignon.*)

rg Coll : Marriage at Cana.

Gallery. Peasants Drinking.

The Bean Feast. J. STEEN, 1668.

.GEN. Gall: David and Goliath. J. STEEN, 1671.

HT. A Feast in Honour of the Election of William III. as Stadt-
en Coll : holder. (*Engraved by Hania.*)

The Dupe.

A Charlatan.

DRESDEN. *Gall :*   Marriage at Cana.   J. STEEN.
                     A Woman Feeding a Child.   J. STEEN.
                     The Dismissal of Hagar.   J. STEEN.
EDINBURGH. *Gall:* The Doctor's Visit.
FLORENCE. *Uffizi.* The Breakfast.   (*Engraved in Molini.*)
FRANKFORT.   Moses Striking the Rock.   J. STEEN.
       Städel.   A Man and Woman Joking.   (*With monogram.*)   *Eng*
                     by J. Eissenhardt.
HAGUE. *Gallery.*   The Alchemist.   J. STEEN.   (*Engraved by J. Eissenhard*
                     The Dentist.   (*Engraved by L. Schweichhardt.*)
                     The Menagerie.   J. STEEN, 1660.   (*Engraved by Zeela:*
                     and lithographed by Last.)
                     A Doctor's Feeling a Young Lady's Pulse.   J. STEEN.
                     graved by Oortman, by Réveil, and by Zeelander.)
                     The Doctor's Visit.   J. STEEN.   (*Engraved by Zeeland:*
                     Avril, the elder, and by Réveil ; and lithographed by
                     der Meulen)
                     The Family of Jan Steen. [*Bearing the inscription* ".
                     ouden songen, so pypen de jonghen"—*as the old ones*
                     so the young ones pipe—and signed, STEEN.]   (*Engra*
                     Le Villain, by Oortman as " *Les plaisirs de chaque*
                     and by Zeelander ; lithographed by Last.)
                     The Tavern.   J. STEEN.   [*Sometimes called* "*The*
                     Feast," *but generally known, without reason, as* "*I.*
                     Humaine."]   (*Engraved by Oortman, by Réveil, a:*
                     Zeelander ; and lithographed by Last.)
    Steengracht Coll : Portraits of Jan Steen and his Family.
                     The Doctor's Visit.   (*Engraved by A. de Bloys.*)
                     A Merry Company.
V. de Wynpersse C. A Merry Gathering.
LONDON. *Nat: Gall:* The Music-master.   JOHANIS STEEN FECIT, 16— (1671 ?
    Apsley House.   The Doctor's Visit—the Invalid Lady.
                     A Merry Company.
                     The Effects of Intemperance.
  Ashburton Coll : Playing at Skittles.
  Bridgewater Ho : A School.
                     Selling Fish.
     Bute Coll :   Cocks Fighting.
                     A Farm Pillaged.
                     Bathsheba.
                     The Musicians.

ngham Pal :	The Toilet. J. STEEN, 1663.
	Peasants Dancing, Singing, and Drinking.
	Peasants Quarrelling. (*Dated* 1672.)
	The Feast.
	A Village Inn.
	The Card Players. J. STEEN.
ford House.	The Christening Feast. J. STEEN, 1654.
lbrook Coll :	The Skittle Players. (*Engraved by De Ghend.*)
	Portrait of Steen. (*Engraved by C. W. Marr.*)
	A School.
	A Village Wedding.
	A Merry Company.
	Portrait of Himself—Singing and Playing the Lute.
PELLIER.	Travellers Resting.
usée Fabre.	A Merry Company.
CH. Pina-	Peasants Quarrelling. J. STEEN, 1664.
kothek.	The Doctor's Visit. J. STEEN.
ES. *Mus;*	The Topers.
. *Louvre.*	A Feast in a Flemish Inn. (*Dated* 1674.)
. *Gallery.*	Peasants Carousing. (*Signed.*)
RDAM.	
uyzen Coll :	An Interior ; Peasants.
Bruyn Coll :	Esther before Ahasuerus. (*Similar to the picture in the Hermitage, St. Petersburg.*)
Museum.	The Fête of St. Nicholas. JAN STEEN.
	The Sham Operation. J. STEEN.
s. Museum.	" Amours de Jan Steen."
TERSBURG.	Esther before Ahasuerus.
Hermitage.	The Doctor's Visit.
	A Summer Fête in a Garden.
	The Drinkers—*a Man Smoking, and a Woman Asleep.*
	The Old Invalid.
	The Backgammon Players. [*The Man, Playing with the Lady, represents Jan Steen himself.*] (*Signed and dated* 1667.)
	A Peasant Wedding. (*Signed.*)
	Interior of a Cabaret. (*Signed.*)
E. Academy.	An Interior, with Figures.
A. Belvedere.	A Peasant Wedding.
	Peasants Drinking. (*Painted in* 1663.)
SOR CASTLE.	An Interior.

GABRIEL METSU. ꞹM

AMSTERDAM.	The Breakfast. G. METSU. (*Engraved by D. J. Sluyter*
Museum.	The Old Toper. (*Engraved by J. P. Lange, and etch J. A. Boland.*)
Van der Hoop C.	A Huntsman Presenting a Partridge to a Lady.
BERLIN. *Museum.*	The Family of the Merchant Gelling. G. METSU.
	The Cook. G. METSUE.
	Portrait of a Lady. (*Perhaps the mother of the painter.*
BRUNSWICK. *Gall:*	A Dutch Woman.
BRUSSELS. *Museum.*	The Collation. G. METSU.
CASSEL. *Gallery.*	A Woman Purchasing Game.
	A Young Woman Seated at her Door giving Alms to a GABRIEL METSU.
	A Young Woman Playing a Lute.
DRESDEN. *Gallery.*	A Man and his Wife in an Ale-house. G. METSU, 1661.
	An Old Poultry-seller Offering a Fowl to a Young G. METSU, 1662.
	An Old Woman, bargaining with a Poultry-woman. G. ꞵ 1662. (*With the inscription* VRIJE VERKOPING HOF MAERSEN—*the name of a village between Amsterda Utrecht; where Metsu probably had a country house.*)
	The Game-seller, Bargaining with a Cook. G. METSU.
	A Man Smoking by a Fire. G. METSU.
	A Young Woman with a Lace Cushion in her Lap. G. ꞵ
	A Young Woman Reading a Letter.
FLORENCE. *Uffizi.*	Domestic Scene—*a Lady Playing a Guitar and a Litt Playing with a Dog.* (*Engraved in Molini.*)
	A Lady and a Cavalier. (*Engraved in Molini.*)
HAGUE. *Gallery.*	The Huntsman—*a portrait.* G. METSU, 1661. (*Engra Chataigner, Zeelander, C. C. A. Last, and in rece A. C. Nunnink.*)
	The Amateur Musicians. G. METSU. (*Engraved by Chat Watson, Huijgens, and C. C. A. Last.*)
	Justice Protecting the Widow and the Orphan. G. (*Lithographed by Elink Sterk.*)

N. *Nation-* The Duet. G. METSU. (*Engraved in the "Choiseul Gallery."*)
l Gallery. The Music Lesson. G. METSU.
       The Drowsy Landlady. G. METSU.
rton Coll: Bust of an Old Woman in a Window. G. METSU.
       A Girl Drawing from a Bust.
water Ho: The Fish-wife. G. METSU.
       A Lady Caressing her Lap-dog.
       The Stirrup Cup.
gham Pal: A Lady with a Wine-glass.
       A Man Playing on a Violoncello, and a Lady. METSU.
       A Lady and a Guitar-player.
       The Artist Painting. G. METSU.
rook Coll: The Intruder.
D. *Gall:* A Dead Hen.
'ELLIER. The Writer.
usée Fabre. Fisherwoman.
M. *Pina-* A Cook with a Fowl. G. METSU.
kothek. A Feast. G. METSU.
Louvre. The Woman taken in Adultery. G. METSU A°, 1653.
       The Vegetable Market at Amsterdam. METSU. (*Engraved by David, and in Filhol.*)
       An Officer Entertaining a Young Lady. (*Engraved by Audouin, and in Filhol.*)
       The Music Lesson. G. METSU. (*Engraved in Filhol.*)
       The Chemist at a Window. METSU. (*Engraved in Filhol.*)
       A Dutch Woman. (*Engraved by J. Daullé as "La Riboteuse;" by Oortman, and in Filhol.*)
       A Dutch Cook. G. METSU. (*Engraved by J. Daullé as "La Peleuse de pommes;' by Massard, and in Filhol.*)
       Portrait of Admiral Cornelis van Tromp.
. Gallery. A Man and a Lady.
RDAM. *Mus:* A Priest in his Study.
TERSBURG. Interior of a Public-house (*known as the "Prodigal Son."*)
Hermitage. The Sick Woman. (*Signed and dated* 1637.)
       The Concert.
       The Breakfast of Oysters.
       The Repast.
A. *Belvedere.* The Lace-maker.
ernin Coll: The Smoker.

NICOLAAS MAES.

AMSTERDAM.	The Dreamer. N. MAAS. (*Engraved by J. P. Lange.*)
Museum.	A Woman Spinning. N. MES. (*Etched by Unger.*)
Van der Hoop C.	A Woman Spinning.
Six Coll :	The Eavesdropper.
BERLIN. *Museum.*	A Philosopher. (*Formerly ascribed to Bol : doubtful.*)
BRUSSELS. *Mus :*	A Woman Reading.
COPENHAGEN.	Portrait of Man. N. MAAS.
Gallery.	Portrait of a Lady.
DRESDEN. *Gall :*	Two Women in a Kitchen. N. MAES.
	Portrait of Baron Godard van Reede-Agrim.
	Graf von Athlone, Herr of Ameronghen. MAES, 1676.
HAGUE. *Gallery.*	Portrait of a Man, *clothed in black.* ÆT. 84. N. MAES, 1
	Diana and Nymphs, Bathing. N. M., 1650.
Steengracht Coll :	An Interior.
LONDON. *Nat.*	The Cradle. (*With monogram.*)
Gall :	The Dutch House-wife. N. MAES, 1655.
	The Idle Servant. N. MAES, 1655.
Apsley House.	Selling Milk.
	A Girl Listening.
Bridgewater Ho :	A Girl Threading her Needle. N. MAES. 1657.
Buckingham Pal :	A Girl Listening. N. MES. A. 1665.
Hertford House.	A Boy on Horseback.
	The Servant on the Stair. (*Dated* 1656.)
MUNICH. *Pina-*	Portrait of a Young Man, in a landscape.
kothek.	Portrait of a Young Woman, in a landscape.
PESTH. *Gallery.*	Portrait of a Man.
ROTTERDAM. *Mus :*	A Gentleman and his Wife and Child. N. MAES.
	Portrait of Willem Nieuwport.
	Portrait of his Wife. N. MAES, 1672.
ST. PETERSBURG.	An Interior, *a mother with her children.*
Hermitage.	A Woman fallen asleep while winding Thread.

JAN VER MEER, OF DELFT.   ⨈

AMSTERDAM.	
Six Coll :	Woman Pouring out Milk.
	View of a Street. I. V. MEER.
Van der Hoop C.	Woman Reading.

ıN. *Museum.* A House in the Country. (*Early work.*)

Boy Blowing Bubbles. (*Early work.*)

The Girl with the Pearl Necklace. ı. v. MEER. (*Late work.*)

SWICK. *Gall.* The Coquette ("The Girl with the Drinking Glass.")

SELS.

nberg Coll : A Young Girl.

ıEN. *Gallery.* Interior, *a man embracing a girl.* ı. VAN MEER, 1656. (*The only life-size painting known by the master.*)

A Girl Reading a Letter at an Open Window. ı. v. MEER.

ıE. *Gallery.* View of Delft, taken from the Rotterdam Canal. (*With monogram given above*) (*Engraved by Huijgens, lithographed by W. J. J. Nuijen.*) *A study for this picture is in the Museum at Frankfort ; it has been etched by Lalanne.*

ı. *Gallery.* An Interior.

S. *Louvre.* The Lace-maker. ı. MEER.

ıı. *Gallery.* Still Life.

'ETERSBURG. Still Life. (*In the Hermitage.*)

NA. *Academy.* A Dutch Family.

ıSOR CASTLE. A Lady Playing a Spinet. ı. v. MEER.

PIETER DE HOOCH. Ⱶ

ıERDAM. *Mus:* Portrait of Himself. ÆTATIS 19. (*With monogram given above.*)

The Buttery-hatch. ı. D. ıı. (*Etched by Boland and by Unger.*)

der Hoop C. Morning Toilet.—*And others.*

Six Coll : The Linen-press.

ıN. *Mus:* A Dutch Interior—*mother and child.* (*A master-piece.*)

ıNHAGEN. Persons Playing and Dancing. ı. D. HOOCH.

Gallery. A Family Concert. ı. D. HOOCH.

An Interior. —ıı—

ıKFORT. A Lady at her Writing-table. ı. DE HOOGH. (*In the Städel.*)

UE. Musical Party. (*In the Steengracht Collection.*)

ı. *Gallery.* Dutch Interior.

ıON. *National Gallery.* The Courtyard of a Dutch House—*a house-wife speaking to her maid-servant.* ı. D. ıı., 1665.

An Interior—*two gentlemen conversing with a lady.* ı. D. ıı.

Courtyard of a Dutch House, Paved with Bricks. ı. D. ıı. A° 1658.

Apsley House.   A Lady at her Toilet.
Ashburton Coll: A Woman and a Child walking in a street of Utrecht.
Buckingham Pal: A Courtyard.   P. D. HOOCH.
                 Three Gentlemen and a Lady Playing Cards.   P. D. H.   1(
Northbrook Coll: An Interior.
MUNICH.   Dutch Interior—*a Woman Reading.* (*In the Pinakothek.*)
NUREMBERG. *Mus:* Dutch Interior.
PARIS.   *Louvre.*   Dutch Interior—*Two Women and a Child, with a meal pared on the table.*   P. D. HOOCH.   (*Engraved in Filhol.*
                 Dutch Interior—*Card Players.*   P. D. HOOCH.
ST. PETERSBURG.   A Lady Seated at a Door—*her servant brings her a fish.*
    Hermitage.   A Dutch Interior—*a lady plays the lute and sings; a cava accompanies her in the song.* (*Signed.*)
                 The Lace-maker.
VIENNA. *Czernin C.* A Painter in his Studio.

FRANS VAN MIERIS.

AMSTERDAM. *Mus:* The Correspondence.   F. VAN MIERIS, ANNO 1680.
                 The Lute-player.
                 Fragility.
Van der Hoop C.   The Grocer's Shop.
                 Pharmacy.
BERLIN. *Museum.* Portrait of a Young Man.
                 A Young Woman before a Glass.
COPENHAGEN.   A Dutch Peasant's Room.   F. VAN MIERIS.
    Gallery.   Portrait of Ulrich Frederik Gyldenlove.   F. VAN MIERIS F
                 A° 1662.
                 An Officer.
                 Portrait of a Man (*said to be Eglon van der Neer*). F. V. MIE
                 Portrait of a Lady.   F. V. MIERIS F.
DRESDEN. *Gall:* A Girl Sitting at a Table, Listening to an Old Woman.
                 VAN MIERIS FEC 1671.
                 The Magdalen.   FRANS VAN MIERIS, 1674.
                 A Lady Playing the Lute.   F. VAN MIERIS, ANNO 1675.
                 An Old Woman Placing a Pink in a Flower-pot. F. V. MIE
                 An Old Man—*with a mug and a pipe.*   F. V. MIERIS.
                 A Young Lady, with a Dog in her Lap.   F. V. MIERIS.
                 A Soldier Smoking.   F. V. MIERIS.

DEN. *Gall.* A Man in a Cuirass, with his Hand on his Dagger. F. V. MIERIS.
A Man Mending a Pen. F. V. MIERIS F.
The Tinker. F. VAN MIERIS.
Portrait of Himself in his Studio. F (?) VAN MIERIS.
The Studio of the Painter. F. V. M.
A Girl with a Parrot.
The Cloth Merchant.
Poetry.
ENCE. *Uffizi.* Portrait of Himself. (No. 455.)
Portrait of his Son, Jan van Mieris.
Portrait of Himself. (No. 890.)
A Young Woman.
An Old Man and an Old Woman at Table.
The Old Lover.
The Drinkers. F. V. MIERIS F.
Portrait of Himself. (No. 876.)
Portrait of Himself and his Family. F. VAN MIERIS FECIT
1675. (*Engraved in Molini.*)
UF. *Gallery.* Soap Bubbles. MDCLXIII. F. VAN MIERIS FECIT LUGD BAT.
(*Engraved by Pigeot, Le Rouge, and Zeelander ; and litho-
graphed by Van der Meulen.*) [*A similar work is in
Buckingham Palace.*]
Portrait of Florentius Schuijl, *Professor of Medicine and
Botany at Leyden.* F. VAN MIERIS FE Ao 1666. (*Engraved
by Zeelander, and lithographed by Nuunink*)
Portrait of Himself and his Wife. (*Engraved by Greenwood,
Le Rouge, and Zeelander ; and lithographed by C. C. A. Last
and C. Bentinck.*) [*A similar work is in Buckingham Palace.*]
DON. *Nation-* A Lady in a Crimson Jacket, *feeding a parrot.* (*Similar
al Gallery.* compositions are in the possession of the Queen and in the
Pinakothek, Munich.*)
ingham Pal: Portrait of Himself and his Wife. Dated 1666. (*Similar to
the picture at the Hague.*)
A Countrywoman. F. MIERIS (*ascribed, by some, to Dou*).
Portrait of Man, Smoking, and his Wife. Dated 1666.
Soap Bubbles.
idley House. The Glass of Wine. F. M. 1659 F.
PELLIER. Soap Bubbles.
Musée Fabre. Genre Scene.
ICH. *Pina-* A Soldier Smoking. F. VAN MIERIS, ANNO 1662.
kothek. A Boy Beating a Drum. F. VAN MIERIS, 1670.

I

MUNICH. *Pina-kothek*.	A Lady Playing with her Dog. F. VAN MIERIS, ANNO 1(
	The Sick Woman. (*Known as the " Sick Wife of Mie painted in* 1662.)
	Portrait of Himself. F. VAN MIERIS, A° 1662.
	Portrait of a Woman (*perhaps the painter's wife*). F. MIERIS, A° 1662.
	Franz van Mieris Talking to the Landlord of an Inn. '(K. as " *La Botte de Mieris.*")
	Interior of an Inn—*an officer fallen asleep ; his wife and landlord.* F. VAN MIERIS. (*In the manner of Ter Bore*
	A Lady Playing the Lute. F. VAN MIERIS FECT ANNO 1(
	A Lady with a Parrot.
	Interior of a Cottage. F. V. MIERIS. (*Early work.*)
	A Lady at her Glass. (*Said to have been painted in* 1670.
	The Breakfast. F. VAN MIERIS, FEC LEYD BAT (*Lug Batavorum*), A° 1667.
	A Soldier Smoking and Drinking. F. VAN MIERIS.
PARIS. *Louvre*.	Portrait of a Man. F. VAN MIERIS.
	A Lady at her Toilet.
	The Tea Party.
	A Dutch Family.
ST.PETERSBURG. *Hermitage*.	An Interior—*a lady playing with a dog.*
	The Breakfast of Oysters.
	A Peasant Woman, with Eggs, *one of which is broken.*
	A Lady Seated at a Table.
	The Guitar-player.
	A Lady Writing by the Light of a Candle.
TURIN. *Pinacoteca*.	Portrait of Himself.
VIENNA. *Belvedere*.	A Doctor Feeling a Lady's Pulse. (*Painted in* 1656.)

CASPAR NETSCHER.

AMSTERDAM. *Mus:*	Portrait of Constantijn Huygens, the elder. C. NETSCI 1672. (*Engraved by Bloteling.*)
	A Mother with her Two Children. C. NETSCHER.
Van der Hoop C.	A Portrait.
BERLIN. *Museum*.	Portrait of a Lady with a Rose.
	The Lute-player.

RLIN. *Museum.* The Kitchen. C. NETSCHER.

Vertumnus and Pomona. C. NETSCHER, 1681.

Portrait of the Markgraf, Ludwig von Brandenburg.

SSEL. *Gallery.* Portrait of an Old Lady (*said to be Madame de Maintenon*). C. NETSCHER, 1670.

Portrait of a Young Lady, with a Parrot (*said to be Madame de Montespan*). C. NETSCHER.

A Young Lady at her Toilet-table, with a Portrait and a Letter. C. NETSCHER, 1667.

Portrait of a Man Holding a Glass of Wine (*said to be the artist himself.*) C. NESSCER (*sic*), 1667.

A Young Lady Playing the *Viola di gamba.*

Two Women masquerading. C. NETSCHER F., 1668.

'ENHAGEN. *Gall:* Portrait of a Man. C. NETSCHER FC. 1675.

ESDEN. *Gall:* A Lady Playing, a Gentleman Singing. C. NETSCHER F. A° 1660.

A Man Writing a Letter (*said to be the painter himself*). C. NETSCHER, FECIT 1665.

A Doctor Feeling a Lady's Pulse. C. NETSCHER, 1664.

A Lady Playing a Guitar, a Gentleman Singing. C. NETSCHER, A° 1665. (*The C and N interlaced as given above.*)

Portrait of Madame de Montespan. C. NETSCHER, 1670.

Madame de Montespan Playing the Harp, and her Son, the Duc de Maine. C. NETSCHER FEC. 1671.

A Lady Nursing a Dog. C. NETSCHER. (*Purchased as a work by Frans van Mieris.*)

A Lady with a Sewing-cushion on her lap. C. N.

RENCE. *Uffizi.* A Lady Winding up her Watch.

A Lady in a Red Dress Praying before a Crucifix. (*In Kugler's Handbook, 1874, this is given to Nicolaas Maes.*)

The Sacrifice to Venus.

The Family of the Painter. C. NETSCHER, 1654.

The Sacrifice to the God of Love. C. NETSCHER, 1697.

A Maid-servant Polishing a Kettle. G. NETSCHER, 1664.

NKFORT. A Boy Bringing a Brace of Partridges to a Man. C. NET-
Städel. SCHER, 1677.

GUE. *Gallery.* Portraits of Himself, his Wife, Marie Godin, and his Daughter. C. NETSCHER, A° 1665. (*Engraved by David, P. Audouin, Heina, and Zeelander; and lithographed by J. W. Vos and A. C. Nunnink.*)

Portrait of Mr.—van Waalwijk. C. NETSCHER, 1677.

Portrait of Madame van Waalwijk. C. NETSCHER, FEC. 1683.

London. *National Gallery.*	Blowing Bubbles. A° 1670. G. NETSCHER. (*Engraved the Poullain Gallery.*)
	Maternal Instruction. (*Engraved by De Launay.*)
	Lady Seated at a Spinning-wheel. G. NETSCHER, 1665.
Apsley House.	A Lady at her Toilet. G. NETSCHER F.
Ashburton Coll.:	A Child.
Bridgewater Ho:	The Toilet.
	Portrait of a Lady.
Buckingham Pal:	Portrait of a General.
Northbrook Coll:	A Mother and Child.
Munich. *Pinakothek.*	Bathsheba about to Enter the Bath. C. NETSCHER, 166
	A Musical Entertainment. C. NETSCHER, F. 1665.
	A Young Lady with her Parrot. C. NETSCHER, A° 1666.
	A Shepherd and a Peasant Girl. C. NETSCHER, FEC. 16 (*Formerly wrongly ascribed to Constantijn Netscher.*)
	A Boy Playing a Pastoral Flute.
Paris. *Louvre.*	The Singing Lesson. G. NETSCHER. (*Engraved by Bittheu and in Filhol.*)
	The Lesson on the Bass Viol. CA. NETSCHER, F. (*Engra by Heina, and in Filhol.*)
Pesth. *Gallery.*	Portrait of a Lady with a Dog.
.	Portrait of Lady Harvey, *favourite of Charles II.*
Rotterdam.	A Family Group in a Park. C. NETSCHER F. 1667.
Museum.	Portrait of a Young Woman. C. NETSCHER, FEC. 1683.
	Portrait of a Man. C. NETSCHER, FECIT, 1662.
St. Petersburg. *Hermitage.*	Portrait of Marie Stuart, *daughter of James II., and u of William Henry of Orange.* (*Signed, and dated* 1683.)
	Portrait of Caspar Netscher. (*Signed, and dated* 1678.)
	Portrait of a Young Lady, *seated in a garden, with a flo in her hand; by her side a boy carries a basket of flow* (*Signed, and dated* 1682.)
	Portrait of a Young Lady, *on a balcony with a wreath flowers.* (*Signed, and dated* 1676.)
	Portrait of a Lady, *seated near a window.*
	Portrait of a Young Man, *standing.*
Stuttgardt. *Gall:*	Portraits.
Vienna. *Czernin C.*	Portraits of Himself and Family.

BIBLIOGRAPHY.

A LIST OF THE PRINCIPAL RECENT WORKS ON THE PAINTERS OF HOLLAND.

BALKEMA, C. H., Biographie des Peintres flamands et hollandais qui ont existé depuis Jean et Hubert Van Eyck jusqu' à nos jours. Gand, 1844.

BLANC, CHARLES, Histoire des Peintres de toutes les Écoles, depuis la Renaissance jusqu'à nos jours. Paris, 1849, &c.

BÜRGER, W. (TH. THORÉ), Musées de la Hollande, Amsterdam, et La Haye. Études sur l'École Hollandaise. 2 vols. Paris, 1858—60.

GAEDERTZ, DR. THEODOR, ADRIAN VAN OSTADE, sein Leben und seine Kunst. Lübeck, 1869.

IMMERZEEL, J. C. H. and C., De Levens en Werken der hollandsche en flaamsche Kunstschilders, Beeldhouwers, Graveurs en Bouwmeesters, van het begin der vijftiende tot op de helft der negentiende eeuw, &c. 3 vols. Amsterdam, 1855.

KRAMM, CHRISTIAAN, De levens en werken der Hollandsche en Vlaamsche Kunstschilders, Beeldhouwers, Graveurs en Bouwmeesters, van den vroegsten tot op ouzen tijd. Amsterdam, 1856.

KUGLER, FRANZ THEODOR, Handbook of Painting. The German, Flemish and Dutch Schools. Based on the Handbook of Kugler. Re-modelled by the late Professor Dr. Waagen. A New Edition, thoroughly revised, and in part re-written. By J. A. Crowe. In Two Parts. London, 1874.

LEMCKE, DR. CARL. Biographies of GERARD TER-BORCH; ADRIAEN VAN OSTADE; GERARD DOU; GABRIEL METSU; ISAAK VAN OSTADE; JAN VAN DER MEER VAN DELFT; FRANS VAN MIERIS; PIETER DE HOOCH; JAN STEEN; KASPAR NETSCHER; in the "Kunst und Künstler des Mittelalters und der Neuzeit. Biographien und Charakteristiken. Unter Mitwirkung von Fachgenossen herausgegeben von Dr. ROBERT DOHME." Leipzig, 1876, &c.

MANTZ, PAUL. Articles upon ADRIEN BRAUWER, in the "Gazette des Beaux-Arts," Paris, 1879-80.

RAEPSAET, H., Quelques recherches sur ADRIEN DE BRAUWERE. Ghent,
1852. (Extrait des Annales de la Société royale des Beaux-Arts
et de Littérature de Gand, 1852.)

RATHGEBER, GEORG, Annalen der Niederländischen Malerei, Form-
schneide- und Kupferstecherkunst. (Von A. Dürer's Anwesenheit in
den Neiderländen .... bis auf Rembrant's Tod.) Gotha, 1842-44.

SCHMIDT, WILHELM, Das Leben des Malers ADRIAEN BROUWER. Kritische
Beleuchtung der über ihn verbreiteten Sagen. Leipzig, 1873.

SMITH, JOHN, A Catalogue Raisonné of the Works of the most eminent
Dutch, Flemish, and French Painters, &c. With a Supplement.
Nine Vols. London, 1829-42.

VAN DER WILLIGEN. Pz., A., Les Artistes de Harlem. Notices his-
toriques, avec un Précis sur la gilde de St. Luc. Harlem et La
Haye, 1870.

VAN VLOTEN, DR. J., Niederlands Schilderkunst. Van de 14e tot de
18e eeuw vor het nederlandsche volk geschetst. Amsterdam, 1874.

VAN WESTRHEENE. Wz., T., JAN STEEN, Etude sur l'art en Hollande.
La Haye, 1856.

WEDMORE, FREDERICK, The Masters of Genre Painting: being an intro-
ductory hand-book to the study of genre painting. London, 1880.

The following Catalogues are also rich in biographical details:—

ANTWERP. Catalogue du Musée d'Anvers. (Edited by Théodore van
Lerius.) Anvers, 1874.

BERLIN. Königliche Museen. Gemälde-Galerie. Beschreibendes Ver-
zeichniss der während des umbaues ausgestellten Gemälde. Von
Dr. Julius Meyer und Dr. Wilhelm Bode. Berlin, 1878.

BRUSSELS. Catalogue descriptif et historique du Musée Royal de
Belgique, &c. Par Édouard Fétis. Bruxelles, 1877.

HAGUE. Notice historique et descriptive des Tableaux et des Sculpture
exposés dans le Musée Royal de La Haye. La Haye, 1874.

LONDON. Descriptive and Historical Catalogue of the Pictures in the
National Gallery: Foreign Schools (by R. N. Wornum). London, 1878.

PARIS. Notice des Tableaux exposés dans les Galeries du Musée
National du Louvre. Par Frédéric Villot. 2nd partie. Écoles
Allemaude, Flamande et Hollandaise. Paris, 1878.

INDEX.

(The Names of Paintings are Printed in Italics.)

www.ingramcontent.com/pod-product-compliance
Lightning Source LLC
Chambersburg PA
CBHW020559270326
41927CB00006B/900